Contents

Introduction

■ ■ ■

Content Guidance

Democracy and participation

Political parties

Elections

Pressure groups

■ ■ ■

Questions and Answers

Introduction

The aim of this guide is to prepare students for the Unit 1 People & Politics examination for the Edexcel Advanced Subsidiary (AS) GCE in Government & Politics. Unit 1 introduces the study of politics by looking at the central ideas of democracy and participation, and by examining the representative processes in the UK. It is important that you gain a secure understanding of these topics because the other AS units develop many of them further.

The specification for People and Politics can be divided into four main topics:

(1) **Democracy and political participation:** examining democracy in its various forms; legitimacy; political participation and referendums.
(2) **Party policy and ideas:** the functions of political parties; their traditions; comparing and contrasting party policies and ideas.
(3) **Elections:** the relationship between elections and democracy; the different types of electoral system; the mandate; electoral reform.
(4) **Pressure groups:** different types of pressure group, features and functions, their activities, the factors that contribute to their success; pressure groups and democracy; the promotion of political participation and responsive government.

How to use this guide

This **Introduction** contains information about the format of the unit test and how your answers will be marked, as well as advice on revision and how to approach the various types of question on the examination paper.

The **Content Guidance** section summarises the knowledge and skills that are needed to succeed in the Unit 1 examination. It provides an overview of each topic and focuses on the themes that most commonly arise in the examination.

The **Questions & Answers** section contains a range of questions which might be found on the People & Politics examination paper. The answers and examiner comments concentrate on the essential elements of the response needed to gain high marks.

Scheme of assessment

The AS GCE has a weighting of 50% when carried forward towards the full A-level GCE. The structure of the AS course is as follows:

D

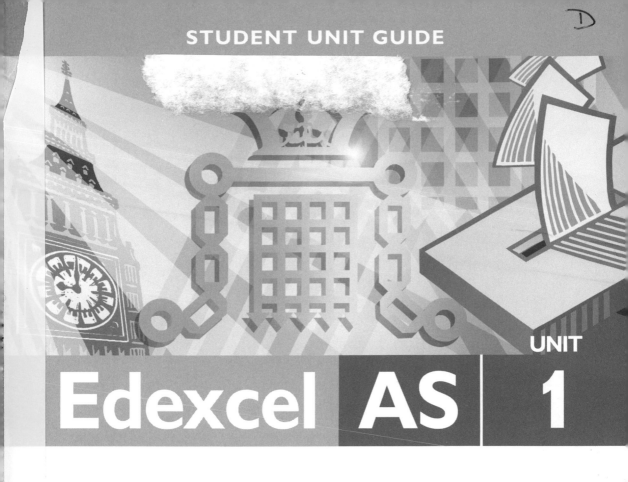

UNIT

Edexcel AS 1

Government & Politics

People and Politics

Chris Robinson

Philip Allan Updates, an imprint of Hodder Education, part of Hachette UK, Market Place, Deddington, Oxfordshire OX15 OSE

Orders
Bookpoint Ltd, 130 Milton Park, Abingdon, Oxfordshire OX14 4SB
tel: 01235 827720
fax: 01235 400454
e-mail: uk.orders@bookpoint.co.uk
Lines are open 9.00 a.m.–5.00 p.m., Monday to Saturday, with a 24-hour message answering service. You can also order through the Philip Allan Updates website: www.philipallan.co.uk

First printed 2008
Impression number 5 4 3 2
Year 2013 2012 2011 2010 2009 2008

This guide has been written specifically to support students preparing for the Edexcel AS Government & Politics Unit 1 examination. The content has been neither approved nor endorsed by Edexcel and remains the sole responsibility of the author.

Typeset by Phoenix Photosetting, Chatham, Kent
Printed by MPG Books, Bodmin

Hachette UK's policy is to use papers that are natural, renewable and recyclable products and made from wood grown in sustainable forests. The logging and manufacturing processes are expected to conform to the environmental regulations of the country of origin.

Unit	Assessment method	Length	Objectives assessed
1	Written — 2 structured questions from a choice of 4	1 hour 20 minutes	1 (50%) 2 (30%) 3 (20%)
2	Written — 2 structured questions from a choice of 4	1 hour 20 minutes	1 (50%) 2 (30%) 3 (20%)

There are three Assessment Objectives (AOs), or sets of skills, that you will be tested on in the examination. In Unit 1, AO1 has a higher weighting than AO2 and AO3. The skills required by each AO are shown in the table below.

Assessment objective	Skills required	Unit 1 weighting
AO1	demonstrate knowledge and understanding of relevant institutions, processes, political concepts, theories and debates	50%
AO2	analyse and evaluate political information, arguments and explanations, and identify parallels, connections, similarities and differences between the aspects of the political systems studied	30%
AO3	construct and communicate coherent arguments making use of a range of appropriate political vocabulary	20%

Exam format

Unit 1 is assessed in a 1 hour 20 minute exam. In this time you have to answer two questions from a choice of four, which means you have 40 minutes to answer each question.

Each question is subdivided into three parts. If you divide the 40 minutes up in proportion to the marks available for each part of the question, this gives you an indication of how long you should spend on each part:

- **Part (a): 5 marks (5 minutes approximately)**
  These questions usually require you to write a short definition, description or distinction. As you only have 5 minutes in which to do this, your answer must be concise. A couple of relevant points briefly explained, with an example if appropriate, is all that is needed to get full marks. One useful practice technique is to find out exactly how much you can write in 5 minutes. This knowledge can then act as a rough guide as to how long your answer should be.

- **Part (b): 10 marks (10 minutes approximately)**

  Clearly, more substance is expected in answers to part (b) questions than part (a) ones. You should aim to make a number of points (sometimes the number is specified in the question), which should be supported by explanations and evidence in the form of appropriate examples, quotes or data. Three of the 10 marks allocated for this question are AO2 marks, which means candidates will be expected to offer some evaluation and/or analysis if they hope to achieve a very high mark.

- **Part (c): 25 marks (25 minutes approximately)**

  Responses to part (c) questions should be substantial — at least twice as long as your part (b) responses. You are expected to offer a range of points that are fully supported by evidence and explanation. Only 8 of the 25 marks on offer are for AO1 skills of knowledge and understanding and recall. There are 9 AO2 (analysis and evaluation) marks. Finally 8 of the marks are awarded for the quality of written communication (AO3). Candidates will notice an asterisk (*) beside each part (c) question on the exam paper. This draws attention to the importance of the quality of written communication in this examination. A candidate who merely offers a list of facts in answer to this type of question is likely to achieve only 6 or 7 marks, given that 17 of the 25 on offer are for evaluation, analysis and written communication. If a question begins **'To what extent...'** or **'What are the advantages and disadvantages of...'** you must give both sides of the argument in order to achieve high marks.

Revision advice

There are two reasons why candidates underperform in examinations:

(1) inadequate preparation

(2) failure to answer the question set.

Some students adopt a very systematic approach to exam preparation: they ensure that they understand fully the principles of electoral systems, for example, before moving on to revise the next topic. At the other extreme, there are those who believe that revision makes no difference. In the middle, there are those students who indulge in 'comfort revision'. This involves simply going over and over the notes and essays of topics with which they are familiar, and putting aside topics which have proved to be more difficult to grasp. Comfort revision is at best a waste of time and at worst will probably lead to serious underperformance in the exam.

A key strategy for using your revision time more effectively is to categorise your notes as follows:

- **Category 1:** notes and essays on topics with which you feel confident and which you understand well.
- **Category 2:** notes and essays on topics with which you feel reasonably happy, but think may need attention before you can answer a part (c) question on the topic.

- **Category 3:** notes and essays on topics which you do not understand and which you would prefer to forget.

When revising, you should allocate time to your Category 2 and 3 topics. You are likely to see a greater return on a given amount of revision on a topic with which you have struggled in the past than on one with which you are already conversant. The idea is to raise all topics up to or close to the level of your Category 1 topics. For this to have any chance of working, you must be honest about which topics pose problems for you and either consult this guide and other books or discuss the difficulty with your teacher.

You should revise all the topics on the Unit 1 specification. Failing to revise any one of them could leave you with limited choices in the examination.

Examination skills

Read the questions

Before you start, take time to read the question paper properly. When reading a question, look for the key words on which your answer will hinge. Consider this example:

(c) Discuss the case for the wider use of referendums.   (25 marks)

This question is asking you to make points on *two* sides of the debate about whether referendums are a good thing or not. If you only give arguments against the wider use of referendums, or arguments in support of their wider use, you will be unable to access all the marks on offer for this question. If you simply write everything there is to know about referendums, you will not gain any extra marks and you will have wasted valuable time. This might appear obvious, but you would be surprised how many candidates missed the key words when this question was set. You should practise identifying the key words in questions on old examination papers. Look out for words such as 'coherent', 'change', 'impact' and 'extent'; these radically affect the manner in which you should approach a question.

Plan your answers

Some candidates write plans for all their answers at the beginning of the exam. Although this takes time, it can be beneficial. If you plan your answer to all parts of a question before you start writing, you can be sure that you will have enough information to answer part (c) effectively. It is far better to spend a few minutes doing this than to get to part (c) of a question and realise that you do not know enough to answer it.

Plans help you to order and reorder your ideas prior to committing them to paper. They enable you to build up your essay in a logical way that is more likely to impress an examiner than randomly stated points. Plans can also come in useful if you run out of time — if your plan remains on your script, without crossings out, the examiner will consider the points made in it and give you some credit for them, especially if you annotate them.

Follow the rubric

The unit test requires you to answer two out of the four questions. Each question is divided into three parts.

You must answer the correct number of questions. If you fail to answer one, your overall mark will be seriously reduced as a result. Similarly, if you answer more than two questions, your overall mark will be reduced because there is not enough time to answer more than two questions properly.

You should be familiar with the format of the exam. Copies of past papers can be obtained from Edexcel after the first examinations in June 2009. Specimen question papers and the subject specification are available on the Edexcel website (**www.edexcel.org.uk**).

Manage your time

Organising your time in the examination itself is just as crucial as good preparation beforehand. All examination rooms must have clearly visible clocks and you should jot down somewhere, either on your question paper or answer book, the times by which you should be beginning each new question. You should then stick to this timetable.

Although it is tempting to devote disproportionate time to questions you know you can answer well, it is not advisable to spend too long on the 5-mark questions — no matter how much you write in answer to these, the maximum you can achieve is 5 marks. This may seem obvious, but many examiners comment on how some scripts have longer responses to the 5-mark questions than to the 10- or even 25-mark questions.

The best way to manage time is to practise. Use the **Question and Answer** section at the end of this book to practise your examination technique against the clock.

Practical tips

- **Do questions have to be answered in any particular order?** No. Some candidates offer what they consider to be their strongest answer first. This approach can help to focus your mind and boost your confidence.
- **Some candidates deliberately leave their responses to the very short answer questions until the end of the paper — is this advisable?** There is some logic to this practice, particularly if you are worried about your time management. However, badly answered questions, whether short or long, will lose you marks.
- **What should you do if there are only 10 minutes left and you still have a part (c) to answer?** If you only have 10 minutes left, the best thing to do is to convert a plan into a series of briefly explained bullet points. Although this will not earn

as many marks as a full answer, it is likely to earn more than a partial response to the question that ends with the words 'Sorry, ran out of time'. It is important to remember that time management is a skill which is being implicitly assessed in the examination; weakness in this respect will therefore cost you marks.

- **What should you do if you are not short of time but feel there are no more questions that you can answer?** One thing is certain in examinations: if you do not attempt a question, you will earn no marks for it. It is better to answer a question badly than not to attempt it at all. Even if you only earn 7 or 8 marks out of 25 for a part (c) answer, this could mean the difference between a grade E and a grade C.

Content Guidance

This section outlines the key content of the AS specification for Unit 1. It is broken down into the four main topics assessed in the Unit 1 test:

(1) Democracy and political participation

This topic considers the key concepts that are essential to understand the basis of politics in the United Kingdom. There is also an examination of the role of referendums in the UK.

(2) Party policies and ideas

The functions of political parties, the ideas and traditions that underpin them, and an assessment of the current Conservative and Labour positions with regard to key policy areas are considered in this topic.

(3) Elections

This topic includes the main electoral principles, the different types of electoral system and the impact that they have in the areas in which they are used in the UK. The issue of electoral reform is also addressed in this topic.

(4) Pressure groups

This topic examines the main types of pressure group and evaluates their activities and the role they play in the UK system of democracy.

Democracy and participation

Types of democracy

Democracy is a word of Greek origin, and literally means **rule by the people.** Democracy is when the people of a state are able to exercise their will in political matters. This expression of will can be **direct** (e.g. when voters express views that will determine specific policy outcomes) or **indirect** (e.g. when representatives are elected to decide policy on the voters' behalf).

Direct democracy

Direct democracy is when all the people in a state make the decisions affecting them on a daily basis. In ancient Athens all qualified citizens were able to decide policy on the major issues that affected them. Citizens gathered to take decisions by majority rule.

In the modern state, however, direct democracy would be unworkable, given the tens of millions of people wishing to vote and the numerous issues about which to decide. Society would probably cease to function if attempts were made to run it as a direct democracy.

Referendums

There are occasions, however, when the people of a state may be asked for their opinion on a specific issue. This process is called a **referendum**. The referendum can therefore be seen as a modern form of direct democracy. A referendum is a vote on a specific issue put before the electorate by the government, usually in the form of a question requiring a yes or no response.

Representative democracy

The concept of representative democracy is based on the idea that, in a large and complex society, it is not possible to involve everyone in the decision-making process. Electing representatives to take decisions on behalf of its citizens enables such a society to achieve democratic characteristics. Representatives may be local council-lors in the town halls or MPs in the House of Commons. As such, representative democracy can be regarded as indirect democracy, as distinct from direct democracy.

Features of representative democracy
Elections
One of the most important features of a representative democracy is an **election**. An election enables representatives to be chosen to govern on behalf of the people and should ensure that the institutions of government and parliament reflect and respect the opinions of the people. In this sense, the political direction that a country takes

will be in tune with the national mood. Labour came to power in 1997 following an election in which the people of the UK demonstrated their desire for a change in political direction.

Elections convey **legitimacy** in that they provide the basis for a government's authority. A government may be said to have legitimacy if it can be shown to have won the support of the electorate. Some critics of Gordon Brown's elevation to the position of prime minister in June 2007 complained that he was neither explicitly selected as Labour Party leader nor led his party through a general election. Conservatives called for an election to clear up this position.

Perhaps a more worrying issue of legitimacy for politicians is relatively low election **turnout**, especially in the general elections of 2001 and 2005, when it fell to around 60%. Can the government claim legitimacy with the support of 36% of the 61% who voted in 2005? (The general idea of legitimacy is linked with that of an electoral mandate, which is dealt with in the section on Elections — see page 31.)

Representation of society

Another feature of representative democracy is that the government (the House of Commons in the UK) should **reflect the society it seeks to represent**, both in terms of political opinion (represented in the views of the various political parties in Parliament) and in terms of the social, ethnic and gender groups of its society. In other words, elected representatives should bear a resemblance to the people who elect them to office. In order to get more women into the House of Commons, the Labour Party has had a policy of all-women shortlists for candidates in many of its safest seats. Previously the '300 Group' of women MPs campaigned for better female representation in the Commons. Currently David Cameron is following in Labour's footsteps in his attempts to secure more women candidates in the Conservative Party's safest seats. All the major political parties are also striving for more parliamentary candidates from the ethnic minorities.

Accountability

Accountability is another important feature of representation. In the UK, representatives must periodically be answerable for the decisions that they make. If they want to be re-elected, their actions need to come under public scrutiny. Elections enable the process of accountability in a representative democracy. The voters of the UK will be able to hold Gordon Brown's government to account at the next general election, which is expected in 2009, but could be as late as the summer of 2010.

Representatives govern

A final aspect of representation may be described in a negative sense. In the UK, representatives are not mere delegates. MPs are elected **to govern as well as to represent**. On occasion, the duty to govern may involve public opinion being overlooked, even if this proves to be unpopular with the people (i.e. if political expedient is outweighed by the judgment of the representative, then decisions may be taken which might anger the public). Many MPs used this argument to justify their decision to support the invasion of Iraq in 2003.

Ultimately, the people of a state do have the final say on contentious decisions; this final say is expressed at general elections.

Democracy in the UK

The table below summarises the points that can be brought into an answer to a question on whether or not the UK is a democracy. Use these points as prompts for further reading or for revision.

Elements of UK democracy	Limitations of UK democracy
• Free and fair elections held at regular intervals	• Elections are not free financially and the government chooses the time of the election
• Political parties are free to air their views and campaign for their policies	• Smaller political parties may suffer as a result of the electoral system
• Politicians are accountable to the people at election time	• Accountability is blurred; most people vote for or against a party, regardless of the calibre of the sitting MP
• The power of politicians is legitimated by the people at election time	• Falling turnout at general elections can call into question the legitimacy of the government
• Freedom of speech	• Limitations on speech regarding race; laws on defamation
• Free press	• Limits on issues to do with national security; libel laws
• Freedom of association	• Some restrictions on the activity of trade unions
• Freedom of assembly	• The police may break up assemblies that they deem riotous
• No official discrimination against minority groups	• Discrimination still persists in key areas such as employment and housing
• Human Rights Act	• Human Rights Act is just an act — rights are not as enshrined as they are in the USA, for example

There is much debate about the nature of UK democracy. Despite the limitations outlined in the table above, the UK is a democracy when compared to some countries in the world where democracy is more obviously suspect, for example where:

- elections are rigged
- leaders are corrupt
- human rights are violated
- people have no say in how they are governed

It should be stated here that these features are not commonly characteristic of most democracies worldwide.

However, some countries appear to be more democratic than the UK in certain respects because they:

- protect the rights of their citizens more securely by having an enshrined Bill of Rights (e.g. the USA)
- place firmer limits on the actions of governments
- have fairer voting systems

Recent developments in UK democracy

Some people claim that the UK has become a more democratic country since the election of the Blair government in 1997. During this time, the government has introduced a number of **constitutional reforms**, which, in the eyes of many on the centre left, have transformed a constitution of the nineteenth century into something approaching one for the twenty-first century. Conservatives would argue that these reforms have done nothing to make the UK more democratic. Indeed, they would claim that the massive parliamentary majorities wielded by Labour between 1997 and 2005 turned the UK into an elective dictatorship. Others, such as the Liberal Democrats, argue that New Labour has failed to tackle the key inadequacies of the UK's democratic system and has merely tinkered with the margins.

Devolution

Labour has decentralised power in the UK. After the 1997 general election, Labour fulfilled its promise of offering devolution to Scotland and Wales. Devolution is where sovereignty resides in a central authority (Parliament in the UK) but certain powers are handed down to sub-national bodies (the Scottish Parliament and the National Assembly for Wales). Parliament retains the right to vary these powers or to abolish the sub-national bodies entirely.

This move towards devolution can be seen as bringing politics closer to the people of the regions of the UK: the reasoning behind it is that the best people to govern major aspects of Scottish or Welsh public policy are the Scots or the Welsh themselves. These reforms mark a break with the UK tradition that political power resides with the government in Westminster.

The use of referendums

Labour held referendums in Scotland and Wales on the public desire for devolved assemblies. Until November 2004, when voters in a referendum in the North East turned down a proposal to establish an elected regional assembly, the government was keen to push ahead with referendums for such assemblies in England. The Blair government sharply increased the use of referendums, and promised to consult the country over the issues of the European single currency and the EU Constitution. The government effectively ruled out introducing the euro, however, and rejections of the European Constitution by voters in France and the Netherlands meant that referendums on the single currency and the EU Constitution were called off.

At the end of 1997, however, the Conservatives and some Labour supporters demanded that Gordon Brown call a referendum on the EU Reform Treaty, which some critics claim is essentially the same as the failed EU Constitution. This increase in the proposed use of referendums can be seen as a move towards more direct democracy in the UK, particularly on significant political or constitutional matters.

Proportional representation

The new devolved assemblies are elected using **proportional representation systems** and it can be argued that the basis for representation in the Scottish Parliament and National Assembly for Wales is more democratic than that for the House of Commons, which continues to use the **first-past-the-post system**. In addition, since 1999 proportional representation has been introduced for elections to the European Parliament. As a result, members of the European Parliament (MEPs) representing smaller political parties, such as the Green Party and the UK Independence Party (UKIP), have been elected. At the European elections in 2004, UKIP won over ten MEPs.

Reform of the House of Lords

One of the long-standing constitutional headaches for the Labour Party has been the existence of the House of Lords. After failing to reform the second chamber in the late 1940s and late 1960s, when Labour was previously in power, the Blair government took the significant step of abolishing most of the hereditary peers in the House of Lords in 1999 (only 92 remain).

This is the first stage of a two-part process of reform. Supporters of the move believe that the hereditary peers were a symbol of undemocratic politics in the UK. Gordon Brown is pledged to complete the reform of the House of Lords, but a lack of consensus on the composition of the replacement second chamber remains.

Human Rights Act (1998)

The government has introduced the Human Rights Act, which for the first time sets out clearly the rights that citizens enjoy. Previously, citizens' rights were based on being able to do anything that the law had not yet proscribed (i.e. so-called **negative rights**). Citizens no longer need to seek redress from the European Court of Human Rights in Strasbourg if they feel that their rights have been curtailed.

The Human Rights Act has effectively incorporated the European Convention of Human Rights into English and Scottish law.

Criticisms of democracy in the UK

Some people argue that the UK has not become more democratic in recent times.

Electoral reform for the House of Commons

The government has changed its mind about a promise the Labour Party made before the 1997 general election: to hold a referendum on electoral reform for the House of Commons. Despite other bodies having new systems, arguably the key decision-making body in the UK remains controlled by a political party with fewer than half of the votes cast in the country. Supporters of electoral reform in parties such as the Liberal Democrats and in groups such as the Electoral Reform Society accuse the government of having only a half-hearted commitment to the issue. They argue that when it comes to reforms affecting the arenas wielding the real power in the country, the government has failed to act in order to preserve more power for itself. Certainly there is no evidence that Gordon Brown is any keener to address the issue of reforming the system by which MPs are voted into the House of Commons than was his predecessor in 10 Downing Street.

Completing the reform of the House of Lords

The government can be criticised for not completing the reform of the House of Lords and Blair in particular appeared to want to resist having an elected second chamber. Given the fact that an appointed chamber always gives rise to the suspicion that its composition is controlled by the government, Gordon Brown remains under some pressure from reformers on this issue, particularly those who want to see an entirely elected second chamber.

Human Rights Act

The Human Rights Act is not an entrenched document. It is another Act of Parliament which can be amended or even repealed at some future date. Critics argue that this has already started, as it was amended almost as soon as it became law in order to restrict the rights of terrorist suspects.

Legislation on identity schemes and the Terror Bill (2008) may also undermine key principles of the Human Rights Act. Many civil rights groups have called for a written constitution containing a bill of rights — they argue that this is the only way to protect the rights of the citizen fully.

Suggestions for enhancing democracy

Lowering the voting age

Politicians of all parties have sought to address the perceived alienation among young people by suggesting that they might support a possible reduction in the voting age from 18 to 16. Matthew Green of the Liberal Democrats has been keen to advance the cause of the 'Votes at 16' campaign. This group campaigned to re-engage and counter apathy among young people. The Electoral Commission began a consultation entitled 'How old is old enough?' in 2002 to investigate the matter further. The Commission reported in April 2004, recommending that the voting age should remain at 18.

The main concerns about lowering the voting age focus on concerns over turnout. The age group with the lowest turnout is currently 18–24 year olds. It has been argued by Phillip Cowley and David Denver in *Talking Politics* that if the voting age were reduced to 16, then the figure for 16–17 year olds would be even lower than that for 18–24 year olds. This, they argue, would reduce the overall voter turnout to levels lower than those recorded for 2001 and 2005.

Introducing compulsory voting

It can be argued that making the act of voting compulsory would result in people becoming more politically active. The think-tank within the Institute for Public Policy Research (IPPR) has come out in favour of compulsory voting. Cabinet figures such as Peter Hain and Geoff Hoon also support this policy. Australia has used compulsory voting since the 1920s and those who support it in the UK point to the high turnout in Australian elections (over 90%). Such a move, they argue, would invigorate politics in the UK and would remind its citizens that they have responsibilities as well as rights.

Not everyone shares the opinion that voting should be made compulsory. The Conservatives believe that forcing people to do something that they do not want to do is a fundamental attack on the rights of an individual. Furthermore, compulsory voting will not necessarily engage people with politics any more effectively. Indeed, it could be argued that the opposite is true: forcing people to participate against their will could foster resentment against the political system, leading to less rather than more political engagement.

Perhaps if voting were made compulsory, a 'none of the above' category on the voting paper would offer those voters who do not wish to choose any of the parties on offer the ability to register their dissatisfaction with the system.

Bringing in 'digital democracy'

Improvements in technology have opened up new opportunities to enable voters to become more involved in the political system. Supporters of electronic voting hope that one day on-line ballots will replace traditional practices using pencil and paper at often inconveniently located polling stations. E-voting could take place at many convenient locations such as supermarkets. Voting from home might also be normal in the future. The arguments in favour of e-voting and digital democracy suggest that greater accessibility to the ballot would increase voter turnout at elections.

Critics of the use of such new technology suggest that the security of the ballot could be compromised if computers are relied upon. Concerns over system failures and the activities of computer hackers contribute to a climate of unease over these developments. Indeed, opponents of digital democracy were given much ammunition after the Scottish parliamentary elections in May 2007, when failures in the new e-voting system led to up to 100,000 votes not being counted properly and major delays in the publication of the final results.

Making wider use of referendums

Until relatively recently, referendums were something of a constitutional rarity in the UK, and there has only been one referendum which has affected the whole country. This took place in 1975 and kept the UK in the then European Economic Community.

Referendums in the UK

Date	Referendum	Outcome
1973	**Northern Ireland's membership of the UK**	The people of Northern Ireland were asked if they wanted to remain a part of the UK. They voted 'yes'
1975	**UK membership of the European Economic Community (EEC)**	The people of the UK were asked whether they wanted to remain part of the EEC. They voted 2:1 in favour of staying in ('yes'). To date this has been the only UK-wide referendum
1979	**Devolution for Scotland and Wales**	A late amendment was inserted into the Referendum Bill (The Cunningham Amendment) which required at least 40% of the electorate to vote 'yes' for devolution to come into effect. The referendums failed to meet this requirement and the subsequent fallout led to the collapse of the Labour government of James Callaghan
1979–96	—	There were no referendums during these years of Conservative government
1997	**Devolution for Scotland and Wales**	In Scotland voters had a two-question referendum: one was about whether to have a devolved parliament or not; the other was whether the parliament should have tax-varying powers. In Wales voters were only asked whether they wanted an assembly. The Scots voted overwhelmingly 'yes' to both questions. The Welsh narrowly approved the new assembly
1998	**Devolution for Northern Ireland**	The people of Northern Ireland were asked whether they agreed with the Belfast Agreement (more commonly known as the 'Good Friday Agreement'). The 'yes' vote was about 71%
1998 onwards	**Elected mayors**	The people of London were asked whether they wanted an elected mayor and an elected body (the Greater London Authority). They voted 'yes'. There have been other city referendums on the issue of elected mayors

Arguments for the wider use of referendums

- **They enable people to decide on issues which they might not have the opportunity to consider at a general election.** Some people believe that there should have been a referendum on the Treaty of the European Union (Maastricht Treaty): in the 1992 general election, voters were effectively denied a say on the issue because all three major parties had given it their official support. The Conservative Party believes that there should be a referendum on the Constitutional Treaty of the European Union, which was signed by Gordon Brown in December 2007. Labour have used the Conservatives failure to call a referendum on Maastricht as a precedent for not calling one now. It is unclear whether the Conservatives will call a referendum if they win the next election however and once again it could be argued that voters are being denied their voice on the issue of Europe.

- **They offer another way for the public to get involved in politics.** It can be argued that voters need to be encouraged to connect with specific political issues and referendums might serve as a means of tackling voter apathy at general elections. The growth in the number and membership of pressure groups suggests that people are interested in issues, and referendums could be a means of harnessing this interest.

- **The associated campaigns can educate the public.** At the time of the 1975 UK-wide referendum on the EEC, massive campaigns by the 'yes' and the 'no' groups were launched. These were accompanied by official booklets outlining the cases for and against the UK remaining in the EEC. For those voters who took the time to read all the literature available, the referendum proved to be an educative experience. It is unlikely that the public had been better informed on any issue since the Second World War.

- **They are democratic.** Referendums are an example of direct democracy. It can be argued that asking the people what they want and then acting in accordance with their wishes can only be a good thing in a democratic society.

- **There are some policy decisions that are so important that referendums ought to be used.** In recent years major constitutional decisions have tended to be referred back to the people. Clearly it was felt that the people of Scotland and Wales should be consulted before devolution in those countries went ahead. The UK's external relations with the European Union (EU) fall into a similar category. There has already been one referendum on the subject, that of 1975, and the Blair government promised (but did not deliver) two more referendums — on the EU Constitution and on the single European currency. Groups such as the UK Independence Party believe that the issue is so important that there should be a referendum similar to the one held in 1975 to determine whether the UK should leave the EU. It might be argued in this respect that the use of a referendum could add legitimacy to a government decision.

- **They can help resolve party splits.** If a political party, either in government or opposition, is divided over a particular issue, a referendum is one way of resolving the dispute, at least in the short or medium term. In the mid-1970s, the Labour government of Harold Wilson was split down the middle on the issue of whether the country should stay in the EEC. The referendum of 1975 was as much about the government being unable to reach a decision as it was about enhancing the democratic process.

Arguments against the wider use of referendums

- **The media could have undue influence on public opinion.** It has been suggested that if a referendum on the EU Reform Treaty is held, the debate will be dominated by the media. Given that the majority of the media are Eurosceptic, it is unlikely that the debate will be balanced, and probable that scare stories about Europe will be prominent among the headlines. Critics claim that important decisions should not be made in such a climate.

- **Governments should do the governing.** The people elect politicians to make decisions and they are accountable for those decisions at the next general election. It could be argued that by holding referendums, governments are shirking their responsibility to deal with difficult decisions.

- **Governments use them cynically.** Some people argue that governments call referendums at a time when they think they will get the decision they want. If this does not happen, they will just have another referendum at a later date, as the Danish government did over the Maastricht Treaty in 1992 and the Irish government did over the Treaty of Nice in 2001.

- **They undermine parliamentary sovereignty.** This is a very strong argument against the use of referendums. In the UK political system, Parliament is sovereign. The forum for discussion and decision should therefore be Parliament. It is argued that the increasing use of referendums will marginalise Parliament at a time when the impact of a dominant executive, the increasing influence of Brussels and the introduction of devolved assemblies have all malignly affected the position of Parliament as the core of the UK political system.

- **People might not know enough about the issue to make an informed choice.** Although referendums are usually accompanied by extensive campaigns with mountains of literature to read, there is a fear that the public will 'switch off'. Given that television programmes about referendums need to compete with soap operas, game shows and reality TV, some critics are concerned that the turnout will be low and that those who do vote might have made up their minds on the issue without too much consideration of the arguments.

- **Voters may not vote on the question posed in the referendum.** It has been suggested that many voters will not address the specifics of the referendum and will instead use the opportunity to vote on an issue more generally. Critics of calls for a referendum on the issue of the EU Constitutional Treaty suggest that voters (and indeed campaigners) would use any referendum as a general stick with which to beat the EU per se. In other words a likely 'no' vote would probably have more to do with people's innate antipathy towards Europe than any specific knowledge that they might have about the treaty itself. Indeed, the Liberal Democrats and some pro-European figures in the Labour Party, such as the MP Keith Vaz, have called for a referendum on the issue of Britain's future in the EU to be tied in with the question on the treaty. This, they argue, would confront anti-European sentiment and require voters to decide whether they want to risk leaving the EU in spite of their misgivings.

- **One side of the debate may have more resources to fund its campaign.**
One of the big complaints of the 'no' campaign in the 1975 referendum on the EEC was that it was outgunned, monetarily, by the 'yes' campaign and that the resources the latter was able to deploy were a significant factor in determining the result. It can be argued that it is undemocratic that one view should predominate as a result of the financial power of its supporters.

Political parties

What is a political party?

A political party is an organisation whose members share similar political beliefs on a number of different issues. These beliefs are usually based on an ideology (e.g. socialism). Usually, the aim of a political party is to gain political power so that they can put their policy objectives into action. All political parties are organised to enable the communication of their messages to the electorate.

The chief job of party members and activists is to gain support for their party's policies. The main political parties have leaders who are normally elected by the general party membership. The leader of a political party is often seen as the focal point of their party and as being responsible for persuading the electorate to support it in elections. This role is crucial and can make the difference between political success or failure. Tony Blair was credited with reviving the political fortunes of the Labour Party (although his critics within the party would argue that this revival began under the leadership of his predecessor, John Smith). David Cameron's leadership of the Conservative Party has transformed its fortunes: by late 2007 they were well ahead in most opinion polls for the first time in 15 years.

The more successful parties, such as Labour and the Conservatives, have seats in the House of Commons. The use of proportional electoral systems has led to an increase in the representation of other political parties, such as the UK Independence Party, in the European Parliament.

The functions of political parties

Making political choices coherent

Parties reduce the thousands of views that exist on scores of policies into a simple set of choices for voters. In this way people buy into a 'basket' of policies that make sense together, although clearly there will be one or two policies in the basket which might not be as popular with some people. People choose to support a political party for a number of reasons, but finding the 'best fit' collection of policies is a key consideration.

Encouraging participation

Political parties play a major role in encouraging people to undertake at least the minimum of political participation: to turn out and vote. For example, at election time parties produce **manifestos** which inform the electorate of their policy positions on a range of issues.

Party membership provides in addition an opportunity for more active participation, offering a broad range of political activities including canvassing, leafleting, local representation and ultimately standing for parliamentary office. Political parties help to mobilise opinion and may encourage political debate. Parties may decide to become involved in campaigns organised by pressure groups by encouraging popular support for certain causes. In the mid 1990s, Labour lent its support to the Snowdrop Appeal, set up in the wake of the Dunblane massacre. Tony Blair himself encouraged citizens to support the appeal's call for much tighter laws on the ownership of handguns. The Conservatives allied themselves with groups such as the Countryside Alliance, encouraging party supporters to campaign against the ban on hunting dogs.

Encouraging political recruitment

Political parties are always looking to recruit new members. This is invariably easier for a party when the tide of public opinion is moving in its direction. In the run-up to the 1997 general election, Labour achieved an increase in its membership. The Conservatives are witnessing a rise in membership at the present time. Parties provide the opportunity for individuals to rise through the ranks of political institutions at local and national level. They provide the state with the future leaders of communities and country. This is especially important when there is no tradition of independent representatives gaining any significant power in the national arena, as is the case in the UK.

Sustaining the system of government

In the UK, the government is derived from and accountable to Parliament. This is known as a parliamentary system of government. It contrasts with systems, such as that of the USA, where there is a separation of powers. In the US system, no member of the executive can be drawn from either of the Houses of Congress. In the UK, it is the political party with the majority of MPs in the House of Commons that forms the government, and it is this party that maintains the government in office. If a governing party were to lose its Commons majority, it could no longer be assured of winning the votes necessary to get its legislation passed. Indeed, if a majority of MPs were to express no confidence in the government through a motion in the Commons, then that government would fall. Parties are crucial to the UK political system in this respect.

Informing the electorate

Political parties provide the electorate with information about issues and explain how a particular policy may be perceived. They raise issues of public concern or, if the issues have been raised elsewhere, they add political focus to them.

Between elections, parties consult with groups of voters in order to exchange views and promulgate ideas. This approach is often employed by parties in opposition, but a governing party may also do so. In an attempt to reconnect with the voters in the run up to the 2005 general election, for instance, Labour conducted its so-called 'big conversation'; this was not only about listening to the voters, but also about trying to explain its policies directly to the people. More recently, the Conservatives have been keen to let the public know just how much the party has changed under the leadership of David Cameron.

Adversarial and consensus politics

There is a debate as to whether the UK political system is **adversarial** or based on **consensus**. It is important that you understand these terms because they are named in the examination specification and questions will be asked about them in the unit test.

An adversarial system is a confrontational system and means that politicians will frequently refuse to come to agreement over issues.

The following points suggest that **the UK political system is adversarial**:
- Traditionally, the ideologies of Labour and the Conservatives have been confrontational, with little room for agreement.
- The 1980s were a graphic illustration of the degree to which politics in the UK can be adversarial — the Conservative government and the Labour opposition (especially in the early 1980s) clashed fundamentally about policy means and ends.
- Parliamentary procedures tend to be confrontational. The layout of the House of Commons, the organisation of parliamentary business and the format for questioning the executive all lead to an aggressive form of politics.
- UK governments tend to be one-party; coalition governments are a rarity.
- The UK has traditionally had a two-party system. In the last 80 years, Labour and the Conservatives are the only parties to have held office on their own.
- The concepts of government and opposition mean that MPs in the House of Commons are either on one side or the other.
- Oppositions are expected to oppose. This is in order to distinguish their ideas from the policies of the government and to act as a check on its power.

However, the above points have to be set against other factors that support the idea that **there is a degree of consensus** (the broad agreement of aims between all parties) in the UK political system:
- Traditionally, there has been consensus about the aims of government policy. This was especially true in the 1950s and 1960s, but it may also be true since the arrival of New Labour.
- After the Second World War, there was even a broad agreement across the parties about the means of achieving the ends. The so-called postwar consensus saw the formation of similar welfare policies from both Labour and the Conservatives.

- Some argue that in spite of the many differences that exist between the major political parties today, there are still remarkable similarities between them on important issues (e.g. on the management of the economy and law and order).
- There was a marked degree of cooperation between Labour and the Liberal Democrats during the 1990s, especially over issues related to constitutional reform.
- The use of alternative electoral systems for assembly elections in Northern Ireland and Wales and for the Scottish Parliament has led to more consensus politics in those areas of the UK.
- A continued rise in support for the Liberal Democrats will accentuate this consensus trend, with further cooperation likely if there is electoral reform for Westminster elections.

One of the mistakes that students often make in examinations is to confuse consensus politics with coalition government. Clearly the two can be linked because agreement and cooperation can lead to coalition government, but often coalitions are effectively forced partnerships based on political expediency. Consensus politics is based on agreement about policy ends and/or policy means.

Political ideologies

The key ideologies named in the Unit 1 specification are conservatism, socialism and liberalism.

Since AS questions are likely to be based on contemporary aspects of UK ideology and the stances of the main political parties, the information in this section is all you need to know for Unit 1.

Conservatism

Conservatives believe in a well-ordered society based on the personal responsibility of individuals. National traditions and patriotism are important to conservatives. They are suspicious of government and therefore have traditionally supported only a limited role for the state.

The creation and preservation of personal wealth and property are cornerstones of conservative thinking. Many would argue that the word ideology is not really an appropriate description of conservatism, since it has tended to adapt the principles outlined above to suit the political needs of the time.

Socialism

Socialism is a broad church including a variety of views on the left of the political spectrum. At the heart of the ideology is a belief in equality, which many on the far left believe can only be brought about by the communal ownership of the means of production, distribution and exchange. The elimination of poverty and social deprivation and the eradication of the causes of inequality are all aspirations that are pursued by people who describe themselves as socialist.

Liberalism

Fundamentally, liberals believe in the primacy of individual rights. Those rights should only be restricted if they infringe on the rights of others. Personal freedoms are at the heart of liberal philosophy.

Historically, some liberals preferred to stress the economic rights of the individual with regard to private property and wealth creation, which has led to some crossover between these 'classical liberals' and proponents of the New Right in the 1970s and 1980s, such as Margaret Thatcher (who was, of course, a conservative).

Summary of key political ideologies

The table below summarises some of the key aspects of the ideologies that are included in the AS specification for this unit.

Ideology	Fundamental beliefs	Examples of policies	Variations
Conservatism	• Respect for order • Individual wealth • Hierarchy • Traditional values • Patriotism • Individual responsibility	• Privatisation • Tough crime policy • Anti-reform • Nationalistic • Smaller role for state	• Fascism • Religious right • Christian Democrat • Republicanism • Conservatism • Evangelical right
Socialism	• Equality • Collectivism • Active role for state • Reformist • Internationalist • Redistribution of wealth	• Welfare • Full employment • Disapproval of private property • Rights at work • High taxation	• Communism • Social democracy • Labour • Marxism • Leninism • Democratic socialism
Liberalism	• Primacy of the individual • Freedoms • Little state intervention • Respect for rights • Reformist	• Constitutional reform • International cooperation • Human rights • Ethical policies • Environmentalism • Localism	• Most Western democracies are variations on this theme • New Right

Conservative and Labour policies

An important debate regarding political parties is the extent to which there is an overlap between the ideas and policies of Labour and the Conservatives. A key theme in politics in recent years is the similarity of the two parties, often expressed in terms of Labour having abandoned its socialist principles and traditions effectively to steal the Conservative Party's clothes.

It is an interesting debate because, like much else to do with New Labour, critics who argue that this is the case are on both the left and right of the political spectrum.

More recently, the Conservatives have appeared to migrate towards the centre ground. The Conservative leader, David Cameron, is keen to portray his party as moderate on issues such as the Health Service, education and law and order. Critics accuse the Tories of repeating Blair's strategy of the 1990s (indeed, Cameron himself is said to want to be seen as the 'heir to Blair').

Similarities between Labour and the Conservatives

The economy

It can be argued that the ideas of these two parties have converged in recent years, that the major ideological economic debates of the past are now over and that both parties share a broadly free-market approach to economic management. The Labour Party's abandonment of Clause IV of its constitution, which committed the party to nationalisation (i.e. the state ownership of companies), was an important symbol of this change for Labour. It could be argued that both Labour and the Conservatives are fighting to establish themselves as the party of business. As a result, Labour has been accused of deserting its traditional values, policies and supporters among the working class and the trade unions.

It is an irony that in the closing days of 2007, the Brown government was paving the way for possible nationalisation of the troubled Northern Rock bank and that while they were not wholly comfortable with the idea, it was not being ruled out as an option by the Conservatives.

Social security

Both parties seek to end state benefit dependency, with Labour continuing the policy of means-testing for social security benefits, which was initiated by the Conservatives. Additionally, Labour appears keen to see people come off the unemployment register, even if this means they are going into low-paid jobs. In early 2008, the Conservatives under David Cameron also published initial proposals to limit the entitlement to incapacity benefits of those who do not actively seek work. Labour responded by suggesting a policy whereby unemployed council tenants could lose their houses if they were not prepared to work. Both parties, it seems, are eager to demonstrate to the electorate that they are tough on the workshy.

Law and order
On issues such as law and order and the sentencing of criminals, the Labour Party has been accused of stealing the policies of the Conservative Party. They both share the view that there is a need for a robust response to crime, and appear concerned to pander to the right-wing press on issues such as asylum and immigration.

Education
The old differences between the two parties over education seem to have gone, with the parties now sharing views on standards and even on the issue of selection. Labour has continued with the testing and inspection regimes introduced by the Conservatives. League tables remain a prominent symbol of educational standards, as does the public exposure of failing schools. Labour's latest flagship initiative — academy schools which are free of local authority control — has been embraced by the Conservatives under David Cameron.

Healthcare
When it was in opposition, Labour opposed the use of public–private partnerships in the provision of state healthcare. Ironically, the only agreements to be signed for private investors to build and lease hospitals and other health facilities back to the National Health Service have been made since the 1997 general election when Labour came to office.

After the 1995 general election, when voters appear to have rejected the Conservative approach to healthcare (involving a move towards private medical insurance for more people), David Cameron has changed tack somewhat. The Conservatives promise to match the spending plans of the Labour government spending on the NHS for the first 2 years after the next election.

Differences between Labour and the Conservatives

There is an obverse to the above arguments. Labour rejects Conservative views on funding state healthcare and has been avowedly **redistributionist** in its taxation and spending policies. Fundamental differences of ideas also exist on the issue of Europe.

Redistribution of wealth
The Labour government has redistributed wealth from richer to poorer families. This policy has links with traditional Labour attitudes and would never be pursued by the Conservatives. Although Labour politicians were reluctant to use the word 'redistribution' early on in the life of the government, many in the party now use the word proudly to draw a distinguishing line between themselves and the Conservatives.

Public spending
An important difference between Labour and the Conservatives is on the issue of public spending. The Labour Party claims to have spent more money on key public services, such as health and education, than any previous government. This has caused problems for the Conservatives in recent times, because they have to prove

to voters that their desire to cut taxes will not come at the expense of reductions in public expenditure. In spite of Conservative pledges on public expenditure, Labour maintains that that there are many Conservative backbenchers who are unhappy with their leader's view on public spending.

Taxation

Although Labour rejects **punitive taxation** to pay for investment in public services, there is no doubt that it has increased taxes. The Conservatives have dubbed these 'stealth taxes', because they are done almost out of sight of those who pay for them. Taxes on pension funds, windfall taxes and increases in national insurance contributions have all netted the exchequer extra cash to fund government spending. The Conservatives tried to make this an issue with which to attack the government in the 2005 general election, without much success.

Another Conservative shift in policy under David Cameron was to place more emphasis on public expenditure, putting off the introduction of **tax cuts** to some time in the future when they can be afforded. Ironically, in the final paragraph of his final budget in March 2007, Gordon Brown announced a reduction in the basic rate of income tax from April 2008.

Workers' rights

Many in the Labour Party also point to how much has been done for workers' rights since 1997. As soon as it came to power, the government indicated that it would sign the **social protocol** of the Maastricht Treaty. This is something that John Major's government refused to do in 1992.

Similarly, Labour introduced the **minimum wage** and has more recently reached agreement with the trade unions on the issue of new **statutory holidays** for all workers. Given the Conservative Party's record in office between 1979 and 1997, it is inconceivable that it would have introduced such measures. Indeed, Conservatives argue that these are the very policies that will damage all that they did to create a flexible and competitive labour market in the 1980s.

Conclusion

It is clear from the above that, although there is substantial evidence to suggest that the Labour Party has adopted some of the Conservative Party's ideas and policies and that, since 1995, the Conservatives have borrowed some of Labour's, there remain clear differences between the two parties. Claims that they are just the same are plainly untrue, since a number of policies have been pursued under Labour since 1997 which would never have been followed had the Conservatives remained in power.

Elections

The electoral mandate

An electoral mandate is a **right to govern**. It is the basis upon which all the decisions made by our political leaders are legitimised: governments can carry out their legislative programme if they have the consent of voters to do so. The mandate is often confused with a party manifesto, but although there is clearly a link between the two, they are not the same. The electoral mandate implies that governments should stick to their manifesto commitments once they have been elected to govern.

There are varying interpretations of the electoral mandate. It can be argued that, regardless of the electoral system in use, the government does not necessarily enjoy the support of a majority of voters. This means that defenders of the first-past-the-post electoral system see no conflict between an electoral system that regularly delivers parliamentary majorities without majorities of the popular vote and the notion of a popular mandate.

Critics of the UK system for electing MPs do not agree with this point of view. They argue that an electoral mandate should convey the wishes of the majority of the electorate, and any government ought to feel that it has this level of support before committing to policy options.

Electoral principles

The main principles that underpin the organisation and conduct of elections in the UK are summarised in the following table.

Elections should be free and fair	Elections should be transparent
• Universal suffrage	• They should be easy to understand
• Regular elections	• Voting papers should be laid out clearly
• Secret ballot	• Counting should be accessible to all candidates
• No intimidation of voters	• The result should be administered fairly
• Conducted honestly	• The result should be accepted as accurate

Elections should be politically free	Elections should be seen to be legal
• Freedom of speech	• Results can be challenged in a recount
• Parties free to organise campaigns	• Results can be challenged in court
• Free assembly	• Ballot papers can be traced
• Press has free political coverage	• Judges should be able to declare elections void
• No state propaganda	• Candidates who cheat should not profit from their actions

Electoral systems

There are a variety of electoral systems in use in different parts of the UK. This section examines plurality, majoritarian and proportional systems.

Simple plurality system

This is more commonly known as the first-past-the-post system. It is used for parliamentary and local council elections in the UK, and for presidential and congressional elections in the USA.

The candidate with a plurality of votes (i.e. at least one more vote than the candidate coming second) wins the seat. The system is a 'show of hands' type of arrangement. Until the 1870s, that is exactly how elections were conducted in the UK — the winner was declared after counting the number of arms raised in support of the candidates at public gatherings.

In the UK, this system operates at both constituency level, when the individual MP is elected, and national level, when seats are taken in the House of Commons. The party with the majority of seats in the Commons (after the results of the elections in each of the constituencies have been declared) becomes the government.

Effects of the simple plurality system

A candidate can win a constituency seat even if he or she receives less than 50% of the votes cast. The more candidates there are standing for a particular seat, the lower the percentage of votes required to win: technically, if ten candidates stand, one of them could win with a little over 11% or 12% of the vote.

At national level, when all these votes and seats are aggregated, the winning party (i.e. the one with the majority of seats which will become the government) often does not have a majority of votes. For example, in the UK general elections of 1997, 2001 and 2005, Labour was elected to power with about 44%, 41% and 36% of the vote respectively. No party has achieved a majority of the votes in a general election since the Second World War.

Majoritarian systems

Majoritarian systems are designed to ensure that the winning candidate in a particular contest has the support of at least 50% of those people who voted in the election.

Supplementary vote

This system has been used for electing the London mayor since 2000. Voters rank their two favoured candidates on the ballot paper in order of preference: '1' for their first choice and '2' for their second choice out of a list of candidates.

The alternative vote, which is used for elections to the House of Representatives in Australia, follows a similar system. However, voters can place preferences against **all** the candidates on the ballot paper.

For a candidate to win a supplementary vote, he or she has to achieve over 50% of the first preference votes. If no candidate achieves this, all but the first and second placed candidates are eliminated from the contest and all of their votes are reallocated to the two remaining candidates according to their second preference. This process ends when one of these candidates achieves 50% of the vote.

In the 2004 elections for the London mayor, no candidate achieved more than 50% of the first preference votes. Ken Livingstone for the Labour Party was in first place and Steve Norris for the Conservatives was in second place. After the reallocations from eliminated candidates, Ken Livingstone crossed the 50% barrier and was elected mayor for the second time.

Effects of the supplementary vote system

This system ensures that the candidate who is elected has the support of over 50% of those who turned out to vote. However, it does encourage parties to come to a deal beforehand, urging voters to 'Vote Smith 1, vote Jones 2', for example. As such, it may promote more collaborative politics.

If this system were used to elect an entire assembly, there is no guarantee that the governing party would have over 50% of the votes. The problem is that not all seats are the same size and turnouts vary between constituencies, as does the size of the winning candidate's majority. Add up these factors across 659 individual results and anomalies begin to emerge; the chance of a government gaining a parliamentary majority without a majority of the national vote becomes distinctly possible, especially if the parliamentary majority is a narrow one.

The system therefore remains as flawed, at least as far as the national result is concerned, as the simple plurality (first-past-the-post) system. Many adherents of electoral reform reject this system because it lacks proportionality and is unfair to some political parties.

Proportional systems

Proportional representation is a general term that refers to any electoral system designed to achieve an election result in which the number of seats that a party receives is in proportion to the percentage of votes that the party wins. There are a number of proportional systems and, depending on which system is used, there can be a variation in the degree of proportionality achieved.

Factors that may vary from system to system include:
- the number of representatives elected in each constituency
- the presence of preferential voting
- whether voters choose from a list of candidates or simply choose a party

The systems outlined below are used for at least one type of election in the UK.

Regional party list system

This system is used for UK elections to the European Parliament. The UK is divided into 12 large multi-member constituencies, which return more than one representative to the Parliament. There are 78 MEPs altogether. Voters vote for a party and the parties publish lists of candidates. The greater the percentage of votes that a party receives, the greater the number of names elected from its list. The UK system comprises **closed lists**, so-called because the voters have no way of choosing between candidates from any list.

The system is also closed in the sense that it is the party that determines the names of candidates who appear on its lists and the order in which they appear (the closer a candidate is to the top of the list, the greater his or her chances of getting a seat in the percentage cut).

Effects of the regional party list system

This system has made some big differences to party representation in the UK. The simple plurality (first-past-the-post) system tended to favour Labour and the Conservatives, because of the solidity of their support in their respective strongholds. Using the list-based system described above resulted in parties such as the Greens and the UK Independence Party gaining national representation for the first time ever in 1999. In 2004, UKIP managed to win 12 seats in the elections to the European Parliament — this would not have been possible without using a proportional electoral system.

The closed nature of the list system as it operates in the UK has been a source of some concern because it gives the leadership of the political parties the power to determine where an individual name appears on the list. This system has also ended the direct link between the constituent and the MEP (in London, for example, 9 MEPs are returned).

There is an **open list** variant of this system in which voters are enabled not only to choose their party, but also to tick the name of their preferred candidate. Many argue that this is a fairer system because it empowers the elector and reduces the influence of the party leadership.

Single transferable vote system (STV)

This system is used to return members to the Northern Ireland Assembly. It uses multi-member constituencies and, like the supplementary vote system, preferential voting (although the voter can express more than just a first and second choice).

The aim of the system is to achieve a proportional result and not just a majority for the winning candidate. To achieve this outcome, candidates must reach a quota in order to be elected. This is calculated by the following formula:

$$\frac{\text{votes cast}}{\text{seats} + 1} + 1$$

For example, in a constituency with four seats and in which 100,000 people voted, the quota would be calculated as follows:

$$\frac{100,000}{4 + 1} + 1 = 20,001$$

This means that 20,001 votes would be required to secure election in this constituency. Any candidate achieving the quota on first preference votes is elected. Any surplus votes over the quota are redistributed proportionately to the other candidates, according to second preferences. If no candidate reaches the quota, the candidate with fewest first preferences is eliminated and all the second preference votes for that candidate are reallocated (as happens in the supplementary vote system).

Effects of the single transferable vote system
This system is the only one that provides voters with a choice between candidates of the same party. As such, it empowers the elector in a way that the party list system does not. The existence of multi-member constituencies is particularly helpful in the Northern Ireland context because of the sectarian nature of politics there.

In the 2003 elections for the Northern Ireland Assembly, 14 out of the 18 constituencies returned members from both the Unionist and Nationalist communities; in the remaining four constituencies, representatives of the Alliance Party were elected as well as Unionists. This means that voters who feel uncomfortable about seeking the advice or help of a representative who does not share their political views have someone else within the same constituency who they can visit.

The system has firm support from the Liberal Democrats and groups such as the Electoral Reform Society. Critics argue that it is unduly complicated and lacks transparency, but this view is hotly denied by supporters who point to those countries where it is used with some success. The Republic of Ireland has operated this system in elections since 1922.

Additional member system (AMS)
This system is best known for its use in Germany, but a variation of it is used to elect the Scottish Parliament and the National Assembly for Wales.

Voters have two votes: one for a party, and one for a candidate in a constituency. The candidates are elected using the simple plurality (first-past-the-post) system. The party seats are allocated using the party list system.

This is the only system that results in two different types of representative being elected. One represents a specific body of people in a geographically defined area. The other has no such constituency to represent.

Effects of the additional member system

Elections to the Scottish Parliament and the National Assembly for Wales elect not only representatives, but also governing administrations. In Wales, Labour tried to maintain itself in office as a 'minority' administration (i.e. without having a majority of seats in the assembly). This came to grief with the resignation of the first minister, Alun Michael, in February 2000.

In Scotland, Labour and the Liberal Democrats have worked well in coalition governments since the first elections in 1999. This has led to some interesting policy divergences with London over issues such as university tuition fees. Since the most recent elections to the devolved assemblies in 2003, Labour has once again tried to govern as a minority administration in Wales, but in Scotland the Labour–Liberal Democrat coalition has continued.

It could be argued that the additional member system makes minority governments more likely, but this is a complicated issue. Traditionally, Labour was able to dominate the political scene in Scotland and Wales. If devolution had happened 30 or 40 years ago, it is likely that, even using the additional member system, Labour would have governed in both Scotland and Wales with majorities. However, voting patterns have changed, and the rise of nationalist parties has meant that in Scotland, Labour has needed to form a coalition with another party. Following the Scottish parliamentary elections in 2007, the Scottish National Party (SNP) governed as a minority administration. Even in Wales, where Labour has remained stronger, the party has recently been forced to form a coalition administration with the Welsh Nationals.

Small parties often do well as a consequence of proportional electoral systems, and this can be seen in the election of members of the Scottish Socialist Party to the Scottish Parliament. Perhaps a more surprising beneficiary was the Conservative Party, which is opposed to proportional representation. In the UK Westminster elections of 1997, it won no seats in Scotland, despite polling more than 20% of the vote there. However, the Conservatives did win seats in the Scottish Parliament in both the 1999 and 2003 elections, which were elected using a proportional system.

Electoral reform and the party system

Type of party system in the UK

The UK has traditionally been described as having a **two-party system**. Since 1945, the Conservatives and Labour have dominated the political system, both in terms of seats in the House of Commons and votes at elections. After the resurgence of the Liberal Party in the 1970s, the two main parties continued their combined domination of seats in the Commons, but saw their share of the vote fall to around 70%. In voting terms, therefore, the UK could be described as having a **two-and-a-half party system**.

The domination of government by the Conservatives in the 1980s, and by Labour from 1997, has been characterised by some observers as **dominant party politics**. Others have argued that, with the introduction of alternative voting systems for elections to the devolved assemblies and the European Parliament, there has been a consolidation and appearance of other parties (such as the Greens and the UK Independence Party), a situation that could be described as **multi-party politics**.

The main point to remember is that when referring to the UK party system, you need to be clear about which feature, institution, locality or time period you are discussing.

The simple plurality electoral system

As we have seen, the simple plurality system is better known as the first-past-the-post system. This system is used for UK parliamentary elections — elections to the House of Commons. It is also used to elect local councils in Britain. For more details on the workings of this system, see page 32.

The impact of recent elections

Many politicians regard the dominance of Labour and the Conservatives, both of whom have had time in government since 1945, to be a natural consequence of the simple plurality electoral system. Both parties have enjoyed periods of single-party government, based on majorities in the House of Commons, without achieving majorities in terms of votes in general elections. Indeed, no party has achieved a majority of the votes in a general election since the Second World War. Figure 1 provides voting figures for the 1945–2005 general elections. It shows that while the two main parties may have dominated the political arena up until 1970, since this time the figures have not been as clear cut — the popularity of the Conservatives and Labour is seen to decrease and that of the Liberals/Liberal Democrats to increase.

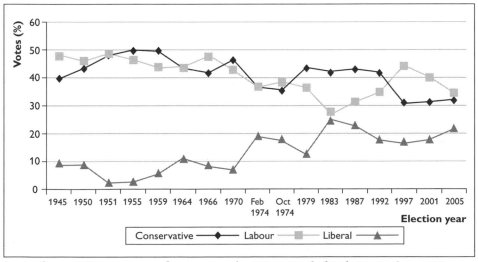

Figure 1 Percentage of votes won in UK general elections, 1945–2005

A different picture emerges when the figures for votes are replaced by the number of seats gained. Figure 2 provides a graphic illustration of how Liberal Democrat votes (shown in the bottom line of Figure 1 above) failed to convert into seats in successive general elections. First the Liberals, then the Liberal–SDP Alliance (1981–88) and, latterly, the Liberal Democrats (from 1988) failed to make inroads consistent with their level of popular support. By concentrating the party's electoral machine on a number of target seats, the Liberal Democrats did manage to improve their performance (in terms of seats) in the 1997 election. They were able to more than double their representation in the Commons (paradoxically, on a reduced vote, compared to their 1992 performance).

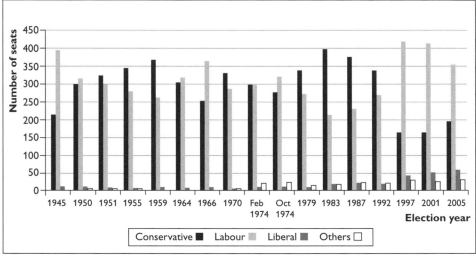

Figure 2 Number of seats won by each party in UK general elections, 1945–2005

Arguments in favour of retaining the simple plurality system

- **The UK is normally characterised as having a strong and stable political system.** This, it may be argued, derives partially from the simple plurality electoral system. Most UK governments remain in office until they want to call an election, with terms lasting, on average, 4 years. They are usually able to get their legislative programme through Parliament and it is rare for them to lose legislation in the House of Commons. It is almost unheard of for governments to be defeated in votes of confidence in the Commons (the only time since 1945 was in March 1979, when the Callaghan Labour government fell).

This contrasts historically with other countries where political instability has been the norm. From 1945, Italy, for example, had scores of different governments until changes were made to its proportional electoral system in the mid 1990s. Such a rapid turnover of governments can often prevent successful enactment of an electoral programme.

There is an argument, therefore, that stability is based on the holding of regular elections at relatively infrequent intervals. Furthermore, this stability ensures strong government, i.e. one that is able to get its manifesto commitments enacted into law.

- **The simple plurality system usually facilitates a single party with a parliamentary majority.** Consequently, it is common to characterise the UK system of government as being single party in nature and the simple plurality system as facilitating this state of affairs. Since the beginning of the twentieth century, there have been only $13\frac{1}{2}$ years of coalition government in the UK, $8\frac{1}{2}$ of which occurred during the First and Second World Wars.

  This contrasts sharply with many other countries where proportional voting systems are used. In Germany and Israel, for example, coalition governments are the norm. It may be argued that such governments are inherently less stable than single-party governments because they are likely to be composed of individuals with differing opinions, and disagreements between parties can lead to the fall of the government. Coalition governments may also be seen as less accountable (see page 43).

- **The UK electoral system is easy to understand.** In any single constituency contest, the candidate with the most votes wins the seat. That candidate then becomes Member of Parliament (MP) for the seat and will represent the constituency until the next general election. The system's simplicity is one of its main advantages. Electors do not have to handle candidate lists or indicate preferences on the ballot paper. There are no complicated quotas to determine which candidates get elected.

- **Constituency representation is seen by many as a key strength of the system.** Every constituency has a single MP who is available for consultation about problems varying from antisocial behaviour to hospital waiting-lists in the area. This contrasts with other political systems where the voting system precludes single-member constituency representation.

  It may be argued that constituency representation affords the system a more robust process of **accountability**. MPs are answerable directly to the people who have elected them in their constituencies. This gives voters the opportunity to reward or punish the work of their elected representatives. Indeed, any alternative voting system ultimately adopted for elections to the House of Commons is likely to have constituency representation as a prominent feature.

Arguments against retaining the simple plurality system

- **Vulnerable administrations can occur where governments are elected without a sizeable majority.** Deeper analysis of the post-1945 period reveals a number of instances when governments have had small or no majorities, making them vulnerable to opposition attacks and prone to internal party divisions. The small majority by which John Major's government was elected in 1992 had disappeared by 1997, making this a difficult period for the Conservatives, with parliamentary votes being so close that they were difficult to predict. Other UK governments faced similar problems in the early 1950s, the mid 1960s and the 1970s.

- **The system has not always been associated with stable government in the UK.** Indeed, it could be argued that the small majorities and minorities of past governments have resulted directly from uncertainties associated with the simple plurality system. For example, in both the 1951 and the February 1974 general elections, the party that won the most votes did not go on to form the government. There is no direct correlation between seats and votes. The 1951 election resulted in a Conservative government with a small parliamentary majority. The election in February 1974 produced a Labour government without a majority (a minority government); another election was held only 7 months later. Moreover, the governments in question have often appeared weak. The Callaghan government eventually succumbed to this weakness, bringing about the general election of 1979. The Major government too, post-1992, was generally perceived to have shown marked weaknesses.

- **Single-party government has not always been equated with strong government in the UK.** There were, for example, periods in the 1970s when the Labour government depended upon the Liberals for its survival. Similarly, if the Major government had not had the support of the Liberal Democrats on the Maastricht Treaty, it is possible that there would have been an early general election.

  Indeed, given the broad (and sometimes divided) nature of UK political parties, it may be simplistic to describe some UK governments as single party. The experience of Labour in government in the 1970s and the post-1992 Major administration suggest a single party nominally in power but with factions appearing to want to go in different directions. The same might be said of the Labour government after the May 2005 general election.

  There may, in fact, be no intrinsic benefit to having a single party in government. Other factors may be of more significance, such as events or party unity.

- **The apparent simplicity of the system is belied by the end result.** Although the voting and electoral processes are easy to understand for the majority of voters, difficulties arise when constituency results are added up to arrive at an overall result for the general election. Voters are often confused as to why a majority of seats in Parliament does not equate to a majority of votes across the country. The answer is relatively simple: if a sufficient number of MPs of the governing party are returned without a majority in their constituencies (they could be returned on 10% of the constituency vote), then the governing party in Parliament (the sum total of its MPs) will not represent a majority of voters.

  Another question commonly asked is why, after polling millions of votes (as they have done in every election since 1974), the Liberal Democrats have so few MPs. In 1983, for example, the Liberal–SDP Alliance was only 2% behind the Labour Party, which nevertheless won 10 times more seats than the Alliance. One of the main reasons is that both Labour and the Conservatives draw their strongest support from well-defined parts of the country. Labour normally does well in

Scotland, Wales and northern England, as well as in urban, working-class areas. The Conservatives traditionally do less well in these areas, prospering in the south of England and in suburban and rural areas. By contrast, there are only a few areas where the electoral strength of the Liberals is sufficiently concentrated to enable them to win large numbers of seats. They tend to do reasonably well across the country, building up a huge number of votes nationally, but they do not win that many seats.

In other words, the UK electoral system is not as straightforward as some might claim. When looked at nationally, the results make it seem more like a lottery than an important tool in facilitating representation and democratic accountability.

- **Constituency MPs usually depend on party support to retain their seats.** There is no doubt that MPs in the UK consider constituency representation as vitally important, but how much importance does the general public attach to it? MPs' constituency surgeries are visited by a tiny fraction of constituents. Indeed, many constituents often have difficulty even naming their MP.

Clearly, party is important here. Apart from a couple of notable exceptions in the Commons, few individual MPs have been able to hold on to their seats once their party has deselected them. The norm, in the long term, is that party support is a key factor in determining the success of a candidate in a general election.

The electoral reform debate

The debate about reform of the UK electoral system has gone on for decades. Periodically it becomes more charged, usually as a consequence of the emergence of a particularly gross anomaly in a general election result. Supporters and critics tend to divide along the lines of those likely to benefit and those likely to lose out from the system. Traditionally, it has been the Liberal Democrats who have called for reform. It is they, after all, who seem to have been worst affected by the simple plurality system.

The two main parties have, in the past, resisted calls for electoral reform. Even after successive defeats in the 1997, 2001 and 2005 general elections, the Conservatives remained unwilling (officially at least) to contemplate changing their minds on the issue, despite being significantly under-represented in the Commons. The Labour Party has always contained a reformist contingent among its MPs and supporters. During the years of Conservative rule (1979–97), an increasing number within the party wondered whether Labour could ever win under the simple plurality system and greater support for electoral reform became evident. However, in spite of prominent figures within the party advocating reform, Tony Blair 'remained to be convinced' of the need for change in the run-up to the 1997 general election. Blair's Labour government has, however, introduced reforms for a number of elections following its success in 1997.

Labour's post-1997 electoral reforms

Following the 1997 Labour election victory, there was much activity on the issue of electoral reform:

- Devolved assemblies in Scotland and Wales were elected by proportional electoral systems.
- The 1999 and 2004 elections for UK members of the European Parliament were run using proportional representation.
- In Greater London and Northern Ireland, devolved assemblies were again accompanied by proportional electoral systems.
- Tony Blair asked the Liberal Democrat peer Lord Jenkins to investigate and recommend an electoral system for elections to the House of Commons.

In 1998 Lord Jenkins of Hillhead recommended that the first-past-the-post electoral system should be replaced by a system called AV+. This is a voting system that combines majoritarian voting (similar to the supplementary vote) and first-past-the-post. You can find more information on the workings of the various electoral systems used in the UK on pages 32–36 above. Nothing came of the Jenkins proposals (despite a referendum on the issue being promised). Critics might argue that this shows that Labour remains wedded to the simple plurality system and is only willing to offer electoral reform where it does not matter (i.e. where no real power will be exercised).

The case for electoral reform
Arguments in favour of electoral reform

- **Alternative systems are fairer.** Systems such as the **regional party list** or **single transferable vote (STV)** are fair to all political parties. A party receiving 30% of the vote should get 30% of the seats in the assembly. This applies equally to larger political parties. In Scotland, the Conservative Party has benefited from the use of the **additional member system (AMS)**, which has given it a percentage of seats in the Scottish Parliament commensurate with its support among Scottish voters.
- **More of the votes cast would count.** The outcome of elections using the simple plurality system often depends on relatively few marginal seats. It is in these seats that the leaders of the main political parties do most of their campaigning, often neglecting large parts of the country. Alternative electoral systems can avoid this. The STV quota system means that in the multi-member constituencies that are used, no candidate can store a majority of votes over and above the number needed to win a seat. The surplus votes are, instead, redistributed to other candidates. Similarly, the votes of candidates eliminated from the counting for having the lowest support are redistributed. This ensures that as many votes as possible count toward the outcome of an election.
- **Minority voices would be heard.** One of the main criticisms of the simple plurality system is that larger parties do well at the expense of smaller parties. Alternative systems can help to overcome this. Systems such as the party list enable votes to be turned into seats so that parties can benefit regardless of their

size. From 1999, UK elections to the European Parliament used a version of the party list system. For the first time in national elections, parties such as the Green Party and the UK Independence Party managed to win representation by MEPs.

- **No government would enjoy a majority of seats on a minority of the vote.** Why should a party be able to govern with 60% of the seats and yet only have 35% of the vote? Where votes are apportioned in a fair manner, this does not happen. In countries across Europe, it is customary for governments to be broad-based, often coalition administrations, drawn from different political parties.

It could be argued that this approach is not only fairer to the parties concerned, but that coalition governments lead to a more moderate style of policy-making, based upon consensus and agreement between people of different political persuasions.

The case against electoral reform

- **Weak and unstable governments.** A main criticism of some European electoral systems is that they can lead to political uncertainty in the countries in which they operate. Reference has already been made to Italy which, until reform of its electoral system in the 1990s, experienced great political instability. More recently, in the 2005 federal elections in Germany, an inconclusive result led to weeks of uncertainty over which parties would be in government and which individual would be the new chancellor.
- **Coalitions are often decided in secret.** Unless political parties declare before an election which other parties they are prepared to work with, there will be uncertainty over which parties will form the government and the outcome may not meet voters' expectations. It may be argued that deals done behind closed doors, over which voters have little or no say, can hardly be described as democratic. Again, using the example of the general election in Germany in 2005, the eventual outcome was a so-called 'grand coalition' of the two largest parties, the Social Democrats (SPD) and the Christian Democrats (CDU/CSU) — traditionally fierce opponents of one another. The outcome was the result of frenzied discussions, compromises and concessions. Critics could argue that the German people were landed with a government that few had expected and that no one had voted for.
- **Disproportionate power given to small parties.** Sometimes extreme parties can gain power under some alternative voting systems with only a nominal share of the vote. Israel's electoral system, for example, has been criticised for giving parties of the extreme right a role in sustaining governments in office. Such groups often end up wielding influence out of all proportion to the level of popular support they have within the electorate.

Sometimes proportional electoral systems can sustain parties that would otherwise have little or no power. In Germany, the Liberal Party (FDP) has served in governments of both the left and the right. Critics claim this has enabled it to side with whichever party appeared to be more popular at the time. As a junior coalition partner, it is not held accountable. Rather, it is the larger coalition partner that finds itself being held responsible and out of office after an unsuccessful general election.

- **Some electoral systems are too complicated.** The relative simplicity of the first-past-the-post electoral system contrasts with some alternative voting systems. The single transferable vote (STV) electoral system, for example, uses an elaborate counting mechanism, involving complicated calculations, to achieve the final result.

  It may be argued that complex voting systems are insufficiently transparent and that, as a result, voters may be unsure about the actual consequences of the votes they cast and therefore hesitant about voting. Such complexity can affect voter behaviour in a particular election.

- **Lack of constituency representation.** Some alternative voting systems weaken constituency representation or do away with it altogether. In the party list electoral system, voters choose a party and not a named candidate. Hence, there is no direct connection between the voter and the elected representative. This may be perceived to be a real disadvantage in the UK, where so much importance is attached to the MP–voter link. Indeed, where the system has already been used in UK elections to the European Parliament, many constituents have complained about having no specific MEP to represent them.

  Critics of the additional member system argue that, under this system, a proportion of the elected representatives are not constituency based, leading to a two-tier system of representation and further confusion on the part of the electorate.

- **Too much power given to party leadership.** The list system has been specifically criticised for concentrating power in the hands of party leaderships at the expense of individual voters. Candidate lists are often drawn up by senior party figures. This can lead to the names of favoured individuals being placed higher up the list, thereby increasing their likelihood of being elected. This situation is likely to keep internal party criticism of party leaders to a minimum owing to the amount of political patronage they can dispense. It may lead to a more loyal, but probably also to a more docile and less independently minded, parliamentary party.

Pressure groups

In a democracy a wide variety of viewpoints and attitudes on all issues exists; this is known as **pluralism**. The existence of pressure groups reflects this diversity of opinion. In the UK, pressure groups compete with one another to gain the attention of the government. Some compete over the same issue, but from different standpoints. For example, the pressure group Action on Smoking and Health (ASH) wants to see the government introduce tougher measures against tobacco smoking (it was partly responsible for the introduction of increasingly strict controls on advertisements put out by tobacco companies), whereas groups representing smokers' rights, such as the Freedom Organisation for the Right to Enjoy Smoking Tobacco (FOREST), want to see the government take a more relaxed line and not tax smokers too much.

What is a pressure group?

A pressure group is an organisation whose members have some shared interests or objectives and which seeks to influence the government. These can be formalised, well-structured bodies that have constitutions and rules. Alternatively, they can be seen in terms of movements or lobbies that might comprise a number of organisations or companies.

There are many ways in which pressure groups can be categorised. For the purposes of Unit 1, you need to be able to distinguish between:
- promotional and sectional groups
- insider and outsider groups

Promotional groups

These groups seek to highlight a particular issue or cause. Their members are often driven by a firm belief in the justice of an issue and seek to influence government policy on it. An example of such a group is Transport 2000, which believes in the pursuit of a more sustainable transport policy and wants to limit the growth in car use. For any issue or government policy, there is usually a cause group pursuing a particular angle on it. For example, government defence policy is the concern of the Campaign for Nuclear Disarmament (CND), which campaigns for the scrapping of the UK's nuclear weapons; it also campaigned against military intervention in Iraq.

Sectional groups

These groups usually comprise members who share a common interest. For example, they may all work in the same profession. Trade unions are the most frequently cited example of this type of pressure group. The National Union of Teachers is a sectional group because it seeks to promote the interests of its members, who are all teachers. For any group of individuals who share a common interest, there will usually be a pressure group promoting those interests, for example the National Campaign for Child Support Awareness (NACSA), which provides advice and support for people whose lives are affected by the Child Support Agency (CSA).

Problems of classification

Some pressure groups are not easy to categorise because they could be either promotional or sectional. An example of this is the housing charity Shelter. This could be classified as a sectional group, because it seeks to improve the lives of homeless people. It also wants to raise awareness of the issue of homelessness, and in this respect the group is promotional — that is, motivated by a cause.

Insider groups

Some pressure groups, whether sectional or promotional, have a status that gives them access to the higher reaches of the political system. They may happen to share many of the interests of the political establishment or the party in government. For example, during the Conservative Party's years in office between 1979 and 1997, the Institute of Directors proved to be an influential organisation, while Tony Blair's Labour government had a close relationship with figures in the Confederation of British Industry.

Some groups seem to go with the grain of public opinion — thus they are almost insider groups by default. The RSPCA is a good example in this respect. The NSPCC might also be cited as an example of an insider group; it is so close to the political system that it has even been given statutory powers to handle issues concerning child protection.

Outsider groups

Other groups do not have insider status. They are on the outside and are not usually consulted on policy issues because their aims are not in line with the political order of the time. For example, in the 1980s, the trade union movement definitely had outsider status because Margaret Thatcher and her government were against any form of organised labour. DEFY-ID is a network of groups and people in the UK who are opposed to the introduction of the proposed national ID card scheme.

The nature of the activities of some pressure groups may make them outsiders. An example is those groups that resort to extreme measures to get their message across. Some groups in the animal liberation movement, for example, have employed terrorist-like activities. Governments normally recoil from groups that are involved in violent acts. These groups, therefore, have to depend on persuading public opinion in order to influence policy makers indirectly.

Other groups may not employ violence, but their activities might be regarded as irresponsible by governments, which similarly makes them outsiders. For example, Greenpeace has a long history of using stunts to promote its campaigns. These attract considerable media attention, but sometimes go wrong. In one such episode, the group was forced to apologise after its occupation of the Brent Spa oil platform was based on false accusations against Shell.

Changes in insider/outsider status

When examining the status of a pressure group, it is important to remember that this status may change, as the example of the trade unions makes clear. During the 1970s, trade unions enjoyed a high level of access to the governing Labour administration. Opinion polls at the time showed that many believed that the unions had more power than the government itself.

This contrasts strongly with the situation in the 1980s, when the unions were frozen out by the government. Even with a Labour government back in power in the 1990s, the unions did not regain the degree of insider status that they had once enjoyed.

Pressure group activities

The category that a pressure group belongs to may well affect the activities that it undertakes. Insider groups, for example, might confine their activities to the quiet lobbying of those in the policy-forming community, publishing reports with the aim of getting the government to act on their findings. They might also undertake work on behalf of the government; for example the RSPCA is authorised to conduct legal actions against those who inflict cruelty on animals.

Many groups do not have such close links with government and therefore have to resort to alternative strategies in order to achieve their aims. They often have to rely on influencing those in the policy-forming community indirectly through public opinion. Groups might use public events, demonstrations, rallies, meetings or petitions to attract public attention.

Public opinion is a powerful weapon and pressure groups need to demonstrate that they have public backing for their particular cause or interest. At their most extreme, pressure groups resort to violence in the hope that public shock might force the government's hand on an issue. Terrorism clearly falls into this category. Although there is some debate as to whether groups such as the IRA are pressure groups, there is no doubt that its terrorism was intended to put pressure on the government. Naturally governments are keen to resist causes promoted in this way for fear that succumbing to such action might encourage other groups to act similarly.

Pressure group success

The success of a pressure group depends on its status, on the public's opinion of its activities, the attitude of the media, the size of its support, the state of its finances and how well it is organised.

Status

The status of the group is an important factor. It can be argued that the closeness existing between some pressure groups and the political establishment gives them an advantage and that by definition they are likely to be more successful. However, it must be stressed that having insider status does come at a cost.

To maintain this status, a group needs to conduct itself in a way that does not embarrass politicians and this inevitably gives rise to questions over the true independence of such groups. Some pressure groups avoid becoming too close to politicians for this very reason — they want to maintain the integrity of their cause or interest and avoid accusations of selling out to the establishment.

Public opinion

Another important factor is the degree to which pressure groups are in line with public opinion. Groups such as the NSPCC and RSPCA stand for causes and interests that anyone would applaud publicly and consequently they find it easier to gain the support of the public, media attention and the ear of ministers.

The media

The media are vital to pressure groups. Most groups employ paid press officers and the bigger groups invest heavily in ensuring that their marketing and media relations support their aims and activities effectively.

Size

The size of a pressure group can be an important factor in its success. Governments are more likely to listen if a group has a million members, especially if it has the support of the public and the media. Timing can be particularly important in this respect. Clearly, a well-supported pressure group agitating in the run-up to a general election might be hard for the competing political parties to resist. However, it is not always the case that large groups achieve success automatically. Despite rising unemployment in the 1980s, when the trade union movement represented many millions of workers, the unions were not particularly effective pressure groups at the time.

Finance

Finance is often cited as an important factor when determining pressure group success. It could be argued that richer groups can afford to employ more and better workers, undertake more advertising and marketing, and raise public awareness for their cause more effectively than poorer groups. At the time of the 1975 referendum on the UK's continued membership of the EEC, the 'yes' campaign was a much better financed operation and this showed in the quality (and quantity) of the publicity it achieved. But money alone is no guarantee of success. For example, the Referendum Party spent over £13 million in the 1997 general election and yet failed in its main aim of promoting the idea of forcing a referendum on the issue of Europe.

Organisation

Often it is the best organised groups — which take advantage of an issue gaining sudden prominence — that are able to achieve success. There is little doubt that in the wake of the massacre of school children in the Scottish town of Dunblane in 1996, the Snowdrop Appeal group mobilised itself effectively to take advantage of the tide of anti-gun sentiment sweeping the country in the months that followed. The group was able to use the pressure of the looming general election to ensure that one of the parties would take up its cause, and Labour was keen to exploit what was seen as an inadequate response by John Major's government in the immediate wake of the incident.

Pressure groups and political parties

Key differences

One important issue to consider is how to distinguish pressure groups from political parties. There are three main areas of difference.

(1) Policies

Pressure groups usually concentrate on one policy area or a narrow field of issues. For example, Greenpeace and Friends of the Earth tend to focus their attention on the environment and issues affecting it. The CND devotes itself to issues concerning nuclear weapons, but has broadened its campaigns within the confines of defence policy. By contrast, political parties offer opinions and viewpoints on a variety of issues, since voters want to know what will happen in a number of policy areas, should they be elected. At the last general election, Labour, the Conservatives and the Liberal Democrats all published manifestos that covered issues such as the economy, health, welfare, transport and education.

(2) Aims

Pressure groups, as the term indicates, aim to exert pressure on decision makers to achieve particular ends. This can be done either directly or indirectly. Examine the pressure group activities discussed earlier in this section and consider how they relate to realising certain aims and objectives. Political parties, on the other hand, seek power in order to facilitate their policies and view the pursuit of power as central to achieving their political ends.

(3) Accountability

By seeking power, political parties become accountable because they will have to answer for the actions of those who govern in their name. Pressure groups are not accountable in the same way, and a number of pressure groups are not accountable in any way, in that their leaders are not called to account for the actions of their groups. It could, therefore, be argued that in this key respect pressure groups are less democratic than political parties, although this general criticism can be disputed (see the section on pressure groups and democracy on page 50).

Practical problems

Despite the distinctions outlined above, it is sometimes difficult to distinguish between pressure groups and political parties. This difficulty has been exacerbated in recent years as some political parties have emerged from single-issue pressure groups or movements (e.g. the Green Party) and other political parties have been created with one issue in mind (e.g. the UK Independence Party).

The second distinction, regarding aims and objectives, is also becoming blurred. Some pressure groups put forward candidates at election time to influence the other political parties rather than to gain power for themselves. Perhaps the best example of this was the Referendum Party, which fought the 1997 general election. It called itself a party and put up candidates, but its main aim was to influence official Conservative Party candidates by threatening to stand in their constituencies if they did not back its call for a referendum on the issue of Europe. It even promised to resign from any seat it won, once its goal of a referendum had been achieved. It could be argued that the Referendum Party was a pressure group seeking to influence decision-making players in the political system.

Those groups that are intimately involved with political parties (e.g. the Fabian Society, a left-of-centre pressure group) also complicate the distinction between pressure groups and political parties.

Pressure groups and democracy

One of the important debates in this topic is the extent to which pressure groups help or hinder the democratic process. The main arguments on both sides of the debate are summarised below.

How pressure groups help democracy

They are an added form of participation
It can be argued that pressure groups complement the political process by giving ordinary people an additional means of participation. This is particularly true in the period between elections, when voters may feel that they have little influence over the government, which might have 3 or 4 years left in office.

They are a measure of public opinion
Pressure groups act as an important weather vane of public opinion, of which the government and other political parties may wish to take notice. The parents of Sarah Payne, who was abducted and murdered, have gained considerable public support for their campaign for increased disclosure about the whereabouts of child abusers. The government has made a number of responses to these pressures, including improving the tracking and surveillance of known sex-offenders.

They are an added form of representation
Many groups are not fully represented by the formal political structures of the state. These might be minority interests or even large bodies of opinion. The workings of the UK electoral system mean that groups that have national representation in other European countries, such as the Greens, are not represented in the House of Commons. Much of the 'green' political activity in the UK, therefore, takes place through pressure groups. This is a form of **functional representation.**

They provide expertise and advice
Some pressure groups are so well placed that when they publish reports or data, the media and the government take notice. For example, groups such as the NSPCC have

been commissioned by the government to conduct research on the basis that they appear more qualified to perform the task than any government body. In this sense, pressure groups can act as an important additional source of information and advice for the government. However, not all groups are in this position: insider pressure groups are more likely to be consulted for advice and information than outsider pressure groups, which are less trusted in government circles.

How pressure groups hinder democracy

They are unaccountable

One of the main criticisms of pressure groups is that they lack internal democracy. Many groups do not have accountable leaderships and there is a danger that groups claiming to represent the opinions of many thousands of people are, in fact, run by a small group of individuals. Up until the 1980s, this was a criticism levelled at the trade union movement, which wielded great power at a time when its internal democracy was suspect. In the 1980s, industrial relations legislation was passed which included the provision that union leaders must be elected by their members. Other pressure groups are not covered by similar legislation.

Group wealth

Some pressure groups have considerable financial resources at their disposal, for example the National Farmers' Union. As a result, they are able to employ specialist staff and engage in more expensive publicity and communications. It can be argued that this means that richer groups are likely to wield greater influence within society, which is inherently undemocratic. A counter to this argument is that wealthier groups are wealthier because they usually have more members and should therefore be given a correspondingly greater share of attention than smaller and less wealthy groups. The problem with this is that in a democracy, the voice of poorer minorities should not be drowned out by that of more affluent majorities. Furthermore, not all rich groups represent large memberships, an example being the Confederation of British Industry (CBI).

Activities

Some groups behave in a way that challenges the democratic process directly. Those groups that engage in controversial, illegal or violent activities may be criticised in this respect. Some sections of the animal rights movement have resorted to actions that have put lives at risk or even taken lives; for example, in the 1990s a car bomb killed the child of a research scientist.

Secrecy

A criticism that is often levelled at those groups with insider status is that much of their activity is carried out away from the glare of publicity. The feeling that these groups are exerting pressure on ministers behind closed doors, out of view of the public, has raised concerns that there is a lack of transparency in the way that governments do business with certain groups and that policy outcomes may be decided in questionable circumstances.

Links with political parties

Some pressure groups have traditional connections with particular political parties and this could open up governments to the charge of favouritism. Many trade unions pay subscriptions to the Labour Party and, in 1997, the Conservatives warned that a future Labour government would bring the unions back to the centre of the policy-making process.

Similar accusations have been levelled at the Conservatives. It can be argued, for example, that the Institute of Directors, while not formally affiliated to the Conservatives, has traditionally supported the party in elections.

Questions
&
Answers

This section of the guide provides you with four questions on Unit 1: People and Politics covering each of the main topics on the specification. They are in the style of the Edexcel unit test, which has four questions, each of which is divided into three parts.

Guidance notes after each question outline how to answer the three parts of the question and how to avoid potential pitfalls. These notes are followed by grade-A and grade-C responses.

Examiner's comments

The candidate's answers below are accompanied by sample examiner's comments; these are preceded by the icon *e*.

In addition to commentary on the answers, the examiner's comments identify why marks have been given and where improvements might be made, especially in the grade-C responses.

Question 1

Democracy and participation

(a) What is a direct democracy? (5 marks)

(b) What are the main features of the UK's democratic system? (10 marks)

(c) To what extent has the UK become more democratic in recent years? (25 marks)

Total: 40 marks

e **(a)** To earn 5 marks on this question you need to give a full definition of direct democracy, including some relevant examples. A one- or two-line answer is unlikely to break into the higher mark range.

e **(b)** This question requires both a conceptual response (in other words, you are required to write more than just a mechanical explanation of how a representative democracy works) and the ability to characterise the UK political system. The answer should focus on the attributes of UK democracy — see the A-grade response for clarification. Your answer should also be related to other concepts such as legitimacy and accountability.

e **(c)** Read this question carefully and look for the key words that tell you what the examiner is looking for. The phrase 'To what extent…' indicates that you need to examine both sides of the debate as to whether the UK has become more democratic (i.e. you need to evaluate in order to gain high marks). The use of the word 'become' invites you to discuss both issues which indicate that the UK *has* become more democratic in recent years and other issues which might point in the opposite direction. One of the pitfalls of a question like this is the temptation it offers for candidates to treat it as a request for information as to whether the UK is a democracy or not, and simply to state the arguments for and against. If you do not refer to recent changes, you are unlikely to get more than 8 or 9 marks out of 25.

■ ■ ■

A-grade answer

(a) Direct democracy implies that all citizens are involved in the decision-making process, not just elected representatives. Early examples of direct democracy were in Athens in ancient Greece. Direct democracy is not prevalent today, given the difficulty of involving all citizens in the everyday running of the state. There are, however, examples of direct democracy in the modern age in the form of referendums, where citizens are consulted and are able to vote on specific issues, such as the referendums for devolution in Scotland and Wales in 1997. These are not a common characteristic of the UK political system, nor is there much common agreement on when they should be used. Gordon Brown's government has ruled out Conservative calls for a referendum on the EU Constitutional Treaty.

question

e This is a good response. The candidate begins with a concise definition of direct democracy, and then gives an example of direct democracy in a historical setting and an example from recent times to show how a modern society can accommodate direct democratic principles. Finally the candidate uses an example to bring the whole topic up to date. This balance between a theoretical knowledge of the meaning of direct democracy and its modern practical manifestation in the form of referendums would earn nearly top marks.

Mark: 4–5/5

(b) The United Kingdom is a representative democracy. This involves the use of free and fair elections to elect individuals to govern on behalf of citizens. Political parties compete with each other to gain the support of voters. General elections provide the electorate with a choice between these parties. When Labour came to power in 1997, it was on the wave of a desire for change among the UK electorate. Political parties seek legitimacy from elections.

Parliament is the centrepiece of democracy in the UK. The main political parties try to ensure that their MPs are representative of the community, in terms of opinions and of social, ethnic and gender groups. Both Labour, and latterly the Conservatives under David Cameron, have used all-women shortlists in safe seats to ensure that there is a more balanced gender mix of candidates at the next general election. Furthermore, all the main political parties are striving for more parliamentary candidates from ethnic minorities.

The UK Parliament is accountable in that every 4 or 5 years, MPs must be answerable to their constituents for the decisions they make. Given that the UK has parliamentary government, elections are also the mechanism by which the government is accountable. At the next general election, therefore, voters will be casting their judgment on the government of Gordon Brown. The process of democratic elections facilitates accountability in a representative democracy.

Within the UK political system, pressure groups may organise and operate freely. Groups such as Greenpeace or the Campaign for Nuclear Disarmament offer an additional form of representation to citizens and provide an alternative means by which the government may gauge the opinions of the public.

The UK has also periodically made use of referendums. These have normally been used to settle significant constitutional issues, such as the 1975 referendum called to decide whether the UK should remain part of the European Economic Community (now the EU).

e This response contains a number of arguments, each of which shows a different aspect of democracy in the UK. The candidate explains these clearly and illustrates most of the points that are made with an example. Add relevant examples to your explanations where you are able to do so, as such examples will help you to gain top marks.

Mark: 9/10

(c) It could be argued that the past decade has seen the UK become a much more democratic country. The election of the Blair government in 1997 heralded a range of constitutional changes which many argue have fitted the UK political system for the twenty-first century. Others argue that New Labour, despite its reforms, has failed to tackle the key inadequacies of the UK's democratic system. Some would go even further and suggest Labour has been authoritarian in office.

Labour has been keen to decentralise power in the UK. Soon after the 1997 general election, Labour held referendums in Scotland and Wales on the issue of devolved assemblies and devolution arrived within a couple of years. The government also appears keen to push ahead with referendums for English regional assemblies in some parts of the country.

It could be argued that these moves break with decades of tradition, in which political power has been effectively the preserve of the government in Westminster. In addition, the fact that the government has used referendums is a move to more direct democracy in the UK.

Along with devolution came the introduction of proportional election systems for the new assemblies, making the basis for representation there more democratic than in the House of Commons. Proportional representation was also introduced for elections to the European Parliament. As a result, MEPs representing smaller political parties, such as the Greens and the UK Independence Party, have been elected.

The government has also taken the important step of abolishing the vast majority of hereditary peers in the House of Lords, whose right to sit there was based on birth. This is only the first step to reform, but modernisers believe that the hereditary peers were a symbol of undemocratic politics in the UK.

Finally, the government has introduced the Human Rights Act, which for the first time sets out clearly the rights that citizens enjoy. This means that citizens no longer need to seek redress from a court in Strasbourg, because effectively the European Convention on Human Rights has been incorporated into English and Scottish law.

However, there are also arguments to suggest that the UK has undemocratic elements. The Blair government reneged on a promise it made before the 1997 general election to hold a referendum on electoral reform for the House of Commons. Despite other bodies having new systems, arguably the key decision-making body remains controlled by a political party with only 36% of the votes cast in the country.

Similarly, the reform of the House of Lords remains only half complete and there appears to be some resistance in government for an entirely elected second chamber. It could be argued that the current arrangements in the second chamber are even less satisfactory than before because the government has a greater say over who sits in the Lords.

Finally, the Human Rights Act was amended almost as soon as it became law to restrict the rights of terrorist suspects. Many civil rights campaigners are calling for a written constitution, which they argue is the only way to protect the rights of the citizen fully. The Brown government appears intent on resurrecting attempts to extend the time for which terror suspects can be held without charge. The Terror Bill of 2008 also aims to give the government exceptional powers to change coroners and dispense with juries at coroners' inquests, which, it is claimed, runs counter to the European Convention on Human Rights, which requires judicial investigations to be independent of government.

On balance, despite some misgivings, the pattern of reform over recent years does point to the UK becoming more democratic.

e This candidate copes well with the demands of the question. The introduction offers a broad overview before going into the specific points in detail — this is often a good tactic at the outset of a long answer as it demonstrates a grasp of the 'big picture'. The answer then deals with the specific requirements of the question: it offers a balanced analysis and tackles the issue of changes to the UK political system. It includes arguments on both sides of the debate and the conclusion reflects the weight given to each side of the argument, by coming down on one particular side.

Mark: 22–23/25

Total mark for question: 37/40

C-grade answer

(a) A direct democracy is when the people rule. Democracy means people power and direct democracy is when all the people in a state make all the decisions affecting them. Direct democracy is unworkable in the modern state with millions of people and that is why all Western democracies are representative democracies. Direct democracy implies that there are no elected representatives.

e This candidate clearly has a basic grasp of what direct democracy is and attempts to distinguish it from representative democracy. There is even a brief statement about the unworkable nature of direct democracy in the modern age. The main problem with this response is that the candidate makes no attempt to offer any real examples of direct democracy, either from the time of ancient Greece or from the more recent use of referendums in the UK.

Mark: 3/5

(b) In the UK, the people elect MPs to the House of Commons and every 4 or 5 years there is a general election in which the people get to decide who is going to govern the country for the next 5 years.

Each MP is the representative of a constituency, which is a geographical area. There are over 600 of these constituencies in the UK. To elect their MP, voters put a cross next to the name of their preferred candidate on the ballot paper, and the candidate with the most votes becomes the elected representative.

MPs are accountable to their constituents because if they wish to carry on in their jobs, they have to submit themselves for re-election periodically. This means that the people can pass judgement on their representatives and that they can get rid of them if they do not feel they are up to the job.

e This response contains three valid points that are explained briefly. However, the candidate limits the scope of the answer to the election of representatives, perhaps anticipating a question on representative democracy. Good answers need to look at the additional factors, such as pressure groups and referendums, in order to offer a fuller picture of democracy in the UK. The lack of discussion of these factors in this answer prevents the candidate from being awarded the high mark needed to gain an A grade.

Mark: 4–5/10

(c) It is clear that the UK has become more democratic in recent years. This is because of the policies of the Labour government under Tony Blair.

Labour held referendums in Scotland and Wales on the issue of devolution, which shows greater democracy in the country. It had been 18 years since referendums had been used in the UK.

Labour introduced devolution within a couple of years of being elected to power. The voters in Scotland supported the idea overwhelmingly, although the Welsh only approved it narrowly. Both countries now have their own assemblies, which is more democratic as it brings government closer to the people in the regions.

The government also introduced proportional election systems for the new assemblies in Scotland and Wales as well as for elections to the European Parliament. There are now MEPs for the UK Independence Party. Without the use of proportional representation, smaller parties such as these would not have been elected because of the way that the first-past-the-post electoral system benefits the bigger political parties.

The House of Lords has also been reformed. The government has abolished the hereditary peers as the first part of a reform process that could lead to an elected second chamber. The hereditary peers were regarded as an antiquated part of the UK constitution because their right to sit in the chamber was passed on from their fathers and bore no relation to their ability or worth. It can be argued that, in a modern democracy, there is no place for the hereditary principle.

It is clear that the political system has become much more democratic in recent years due to the many reforms of the Blair government.

e The candidate attempts to deal with the recent changes to the UK democratic system and offers a number of points supporting the notion that the UK has become more democratic. However, no attempt is made to offer an alternative analysis (i.e. to examine the continued shortcomings of the UK political system). This answer therefore lacks the balance necessary for the candidate to evaluate effectively and so secure top marks.

Mark: 11/25

Total mark for question: 19/40

Question Q2

Political parties

(a) What is a political party? (5 marks)

(b) Explain three ways in which the Labour Party abandoned its traditional policies. (10 marks)

(c) Has the Conservative Party rejected Thatcherism? (25 marks)

Total: 40 marks

(a) This question asks you to explain what a political party is. It does not ask you to describe the functions of a political party.

(b) This question specifies the number of ways in which the Labour Party has abandoned its traditional policies. It is important that the rubric is followed here because each way is worth roughly one third of the total mark. It is equally important not to exceed the requirements of the question. It is better to make three well-explained points than four or five points which are less well explained. More importantly, in questions such as these, the examiner will only consider the best three points if more than three are covered.

(c) This question invites an evaluative and analytical response. The wording indicates that you must give a balanced response which considers the changes in Conservative ideas and policies as well as the continuities. If you focus solely on the way that the Conservative Party has rejected Thatcherism, without examining some of the continuities in Tory policy, you will not be able to reach a high mark and gain a grade A. The maximum likely to be awarded for such a response is only 11 or 12 marks, and it could be less.

■ ■ ■

A-grade answer

(a) A political party is an organisation whose members have shared or similar political beliefs on a variety of different issues, often based on an ideology such as socialism. Political parties exist to achieve political power in order to secure their policy objectives. Parties are organised to enable their messages to be communicated with the electorate. Parties have a membership and activists who undertake most of their activities. All of the main political parties have leaders who are normally elected by the general membership. The leaders of the parties are the spokespersons responsible for getting the electorate to support them in elections. The more successful parties, such as Labour and the Conservatives, have seats in the House of Commons.

This response offers a number of the key characteristics of a political party, including structure, aims and activities, as well as some examples of political parties.

question

In addition, the candidate makes an attempt at abstract comment, by talking about ideology.

Mark: 5/5

(b) Labour has been accused of deserting its traditional values and policies in the pursuit of political power. One way in which this has happened is spelled out by figures on the left such as Tony Benn, who suggests that New Labour bears little, if any, resemblance to the party of which he was a prominent figure. They argue that the party has abandoned the poor in favour of wooing the middle classes and, as such, no longer pursues the principle of equality. The party's refusal to use punitive taxation for richer sections of society is regarded as an example of this shift of emphasis.

By courting private business and groups such as the CBI, Labour also appears to have abandoned the notion of public-sector involvement in the economy. As well as abandoning nationalisation, the Blair government nationalised state-run assets such as the Air Traffic Control Service. It has also been suggested that the party leadership has turned its back on its traditional allies in the trade union movement. After being elected in 1997, the Labour government made no attempt to repeal any of the anti-union legislation passed by the Thatcher governments of the 1980s.

The party has also been accused of stealing the clothes of the Conservative Party on issues such as law and order, and asylum and immigration matters, where the Blair government appeared to be particularly hawkish. The drive to increase the prison population appears to echo the words of Michael Howard, when he was Home Secretary in the Conservative government in the 1990s. In this respect, some see the party, or at least its leadership, as authoritarian. This contrasts sharply with the past, where Labour were seen as less harsh and more liberal on such issues.

> 🖉 This answer describes three ways in which Labour has abandoned its traditional policies. The strength of the response is not just to do with its range (the fact that it covers three policy areas). The answer also attempts to put these changes into the broader context into which the party policy fits. The answer is just under 300 words, which should be achievable in the time available. Thorough responses are clearly more likely to achieve high grades.

Mark: 8–9/10

(c) Many believe that David Cameron has shifted the Conservative Party to the centre ground and away from the legacy of Mrs Thatcher, which included a commitment to a free market economy, low taxation, minimum state intervention and privatisation of state-run monopolies. Thatcherism also embraced strong law and order policies, with tough penalties handed down to law breakers. The belief that traditional values needed to be restored was at the heart of Thatcher's policies.

Since David Cameron became leader of the Conservatives in December 2005, many commentators have suggested that there has been a break with this Thatcherite past in a bid to reconnect the Conservative Party with the centre ground of British politics. This move was based on the belief that the party appeared wedded to the policies of the 1980s and that defeats in three successive general elections had clearly shown that the electorate did not support these policies.

In this context, Cameron sought to identify the Conservatives with policies he thought were likely to prove popular with voters in the centre. Early on, he emphasised the importance of the environment and the need to tackle climate change. A commitment to green taxes was a major departure from the past. Thacherites such as Lord Tebbit criticised such policies as burdensome on business and individuals alike.

On law and order policy, Cameron seemed to abandon the very harsh rhetoric of Mrs Thatcher. His 'hug a hoodie' line may have been taken out of context by the media, but it revealed that Cameron appeared to be keen to tackle the causes of crime. In this sense, his advisors claimed Cameron wanted to be the 'heir to Blair'.

Cameron also abandoned the party fixation on tax cuts, pledging that these would not happen at the expense of cutting expenditure on public services such as health and education. Indeed, Cameron has made pledges to make the NHS a key priority. Mrs Thatcher's claim that 'there is no such thing as society' was rejected by the new Tory leadership. The party seems more ready to view issues such as poverty as problems that governments must tackle.

Despite these shifts, critics of the Conservatives argue that these changes are not substantial and that the Conservatives are trying to woo the centre with a change of style and language. Many of the party's recent pronouncements are somewhat vague and have few policy commitments attached to them. Where policy has been announced, little change is detected. The announcement in September 2007 promising to raise the threshold for the payment of inheritance tax to 1 million pounds is likely to affect only the better-off sections of society and goes beyond what even Mrs Thatcher might have dared to do when she was in power.

On the issue of Europe, Cameron remains a robust critic. Indeed, he wants to sever the party's relationships with other European centre-right political parties because they appear to him to be too pro-integrationist. Throughout her time as prime minister, Mrs Thatcher did not go so far in her criticism of Europe.

After the collapse of Gordon Brown's support in the autumn of 2007, the Conservatives have been consistently ahead in the opinion polls. Since then, the centrist rhetoric of the Conservatives has been toned down on a number of issues. In early 2008, David Cameron made remarks suggesting that society should not be too understanding of criminals, suggesting that his views on the causes of crime were either no longer held or never believed in the first place. Either way, his critics argue that his overtures to the centre ground were not sincere. His recent photo opportunity with Lady Thatcher may give some credence to this view.

Crucially it is important that the broad political context is examined. Arguably, Blair and New Labour embraced much of what Thatcherism stood for. The faith in the private sector, the free market, deregulation, privatisation, tougher sentencing and robust foreign policy have all been features of the Labour government. It may be argued that these are the policies that Labour had to accommodate in order to gain power. There are no signs that the Conservatives under David Cameron have any intention of abandoning them.

Finally, it must be stressed that David Cameron and the Conservative Party are not the same thing. There are many ardent Thatcherites in the parliamentary party and particularly in the constituencies. The Conservative Party has not abandoned Thatcherism; it remains a force within the country and the party.

This response covers the main demands of the question extremely well. It defines the concept of Thatcherism at the outset and addresses a number of key issues and illustrates them using contemporary examples. It also attempts to tie in abstract political ideas with the key policies that have preoccupied the Conservative Party in recent years.

Perhaps most importantly, this response addresses the specific requirements of the question by offering a balanced analysis of the extent to which the Conservative Party has rejected Thatcherism. It includes a discussion of the continuing similarities as well as the differences before coming to a conclusion.

Mark: 23 or 24/25

Total mark for question: 37/40

C-grade answer

(a) A political party is a group of people who work together in order to win power. Members share the same opinions and want to persuade other people to support them at election time. The parties publish manifestos and these contain all of the policies that the party supports. The most popular parties in the UK include Labour, the Conservatives and the Liberal Democrats.

This is a limited response which would be unlikely to achieve more than 2 or 3 marks out of the 5 available for this part of the question. Although the answer does include examples, these are so obvious as to be general knowledge. In addition, the scope of the response is quite narrow. The main focus of the answer is on parties fighting elections and it could be argued that this point would have been better suited to a question which asked about party activities or functions.

Mark: 2–3/5

(b) Labour has abandoned many policies since it came to power in 1997. The party has changed its stance on the issue of the unions. Many years ago, Labour governments worked closely with trade unions — some would say they helped run the country. Indeed, some voters believed that the head of the biggest union had more power than the prime minister. Tony Blair abandoned this stance and instead preferred to govern without the unions.

Another policy abandoned by the Labour Party is that of nationalisation. In previous Labour governments there was a desire to take private companies into public ownership. An example of this is the coal industry which was nationalised after the war. Most of these industries were privatised when Mrs Thatcher was prime minister. Since Labour returned to office under Tony Blair there has been no move to nationalise businesses once more.

🄴 This response is weaker than the grade-A response in two key respects. First, only two main points are made rather than three. The answer mentions the unions but the candidate does not describe this subject in policy terms. Nationalisation is clearly a policy and is correctly identified although the analysis is not quite correct if one considers Network Rail. A more recent example of nationalisation is that of the bank Northern Rock, a step taken as a precautionary measure. The lack of a third point immediately loses the candidate a third of the marks on offer.

The second problem with this response arises from the lack of sophistication of the argument. There is no attempt to contextualise the policies in any broader ideological sense. Some historical references are deployed, but overall the feel of the answer does not come across as well as the grade-A response. For this reason the answer is likely to achieve half marks at the very most.

Mark: 5/10

(c) The Conservative Party has made major policy changes since David Cameron became leader of the Conservative Party. He appears to be more moderate than Margaret Thatcher and so it can be said that the Conservatives have rejected Thatcherism.

One way in which the Conservatives have rejected Thatcherism is by attempting to mimic the policies of the Labour Party. David Cameron now pledges to make public spending on health a major priority. This contrasts with the Thatcherite view that public spending should be cut.

Linked to this is the way in which the Conservatives have downgraded tax cuts as a policy priority. Clearly, if they wish to keep public spending up, they cannot afford to cut taxes at the same time. This policy shift is the result of the Conservatives realising after 10 years in opposition that voters prefer increased public spending rather than tax cuts.

Another way in which the Conservatives have rejected Thatcherism is on the issue of law and order. Cameron's call for people to 'hug a hoodie' demonstrates that he wants to move the Conservative Party away from a very strict attitude to crime and towards a more caring belief that might keep people out of trouble.

Critics, particularly in the Labour Party, believe that the Conservatives have not abandoned Thatcherism and that once elected, the party will revert to Thatcherite policies and take the country back to the way it was in the 1980s, with mass unemployment and high interest rates.

This response makes a number of valid points. However, the answer is clearly not as good as the grade-A response. In the first instance there is no identification of what Thatcherism was. The response needs this model in order to assess the modern Conservative Party. There are occasional references to what might have been characteristics of Thatcherism, but these are not provided in any overarching definition. As such, the response lacks the analysis evident in the grade-A answer. If you fail to offer any conceptual analysis in answer to a question which invites you to do so, you are unlikely to achieve high marks.

The other main problem with this answer is that it is overwhelmingly one-sided. It does not consider any continuity in Conservative Party ideas and policies from the time of Margaret Thatcher and so makes no attempt to offer any evaluation. The final paragraph is vague and based upon unsupported assertion and while it might merit some credit, it hardly characterises the response as in any way well-balanced. This response illustrates the important point that, in order to access the higher marks, you must read the question carefully and ensure that you are addressing all aspects of the question in your answer.

Mark: 11/25

Total mark for the question: 19/40

Question 3

Elections

(a) Define proportional representation. (5 marks)

(b) Describe two proportional electoral systems currently used for elections in the UK. (10 marks)

(c) Should the UK electoral system be reformed? (25 marks)

Total: 40 marks

(a) This question requires knowledge of concepts. Clearly you must not confuse this generic term with an actual proportional system. The single transferable vote system is an example of proportional representation. Do not get bogged down in describing the details of a particular electoral system (that comes in the next part).

(b) This question requires you to describe two proportional electoral systems in use in the UK. You should assume that there will be a maximum of 5 marks for describing each one. Therefore, even if you only describe one electoral system perfectly, you will gain a maximum of 5 marks. Most candidates will not answer perfectly; a realistic range of marks for a partial response is only 3–4 marks. From this you can see that it is very important to answer the question asked.

(c) This part of the question requires candidates to summarise the main debate on electoral reform. Given the nature of the question, a balanced response is required. Clearly if an answer only covers one side of the argument about electoral reform, the examiner will be unable to offer a high mark.

■ ■ ■

A-grade answer

(a) Proportional representation is a generic term referring to those electoral systems which result in the percentage of seats won in an elected assembly by a political party being in direct proportion to the percentage of votes that it wins. In such a system if a party gained 35% of the vote, then it would win 175 seats in a 500-seat assembly. A party with 10% of the vote would win 50 seats. There are a number of proportional electoral systems used in the UK, for example the single transferable vote, which is used to elect members of the Northern Ireland Assembly.

This answer contains enough information to gain full marks. It defines the term, offers a clear explanation of the outcome of proportional representation and provides the name of a proportional electoral system.

Mark: 5/5

question

(b) The regional party list system is used for UK elections to the European Parliament. Electors vote for a party rather than a candidate. The region is a huge multi-member constituency. The votes are added up and the percentage of votes cast for the party is translated into seats for that party. Each party has a list of candidates for each region and if, for example, there are ten seats available and Party A gets 40% of the region vote, this means that the top four names on Party A's list gain seats. Clearly this system does not involve small-constituency representation. Furthermore, this system uses a 'closed' list which means that voters are unable to choose between candidates in the same party. This system has enabled smaller political parties such as UKIP and the Greens to gain political representation in the European Parliament.

The additional member system is used for elections to the Scottish Parliament and Welsh Assembly. It comprises two systems in one. Voters have two votes: one uses the first-past-the-post system to elect a constituency member; the other is used to vote for a party using the list system described above. The system is designed to help parties who fail to win constituency seats receive a fair proportion of those seats awarded through the list part of the system. These are the so-called additional members. They act to 'top-up' the seats a party gets to ensure that overall the percentage of seats it receives corresponds to the percentage of votes won. This system means that some members represent a single-member constituency, whereas the additional members do not. This system has helped the SNP become the governing party in Scotland.

> *This answer begins well. The candidate's description of the use of the closed regional party list system in UK elections to the European Parliament does exactly what the examiner is looking for: it states the name of the system, where it operates in the UK, the main characteristics of the system and how it works. The contextual knowledge at the end displays a real understanding of the practical outcomes of the system.*
>
> *The rest of the answer follows a similar pattern in its description of the systems used for elections to the Scottish Parliament and Welsh Assembly.*
>
> *There are just under 300 words in this excellent response which meets all the requirements of the question. This demonstrates that there is enough time both to think about and to write the necessary amount to get the top grade in the 10 minutes you have in which to answer this part of the question.*

Mark: 9–10/10

(c) Alternative voting systems are fairer to smaller parties that in the past have been under-represented in Parliament using the current plurality voting system. Proportional systems ensure that the party's share of the seats in an assembly matches its share of the vote. Elections to the European Parliament show that, using the list system, parties such as the Green Party and the UK Independence Party have managed to get MEPs.

Reforming the UK electoral system could bring an end to single-party government and the domination of the political system by the two main parties. The UK could become more like some European countries with proportional systems, and have coalition governments. If no party was able to command a Commons majority, greater cooperation between the parties could result in more moderate politics. The Scottish Parliament had a coalition executive comprised of Labour and the Liberal Democrats until May 2007.

A reformed voting system might mean political leaders no longer focus their election campaigns on a few marginal constituencies, with many others being neglected. The single transferable vote system does not allow for safe seats as such and enables surplus votes to be redistributed between parties, meaning politicians have to contest for every vote they can in as many constituencies as possible.

On the other hand, the simple plurality electoral system has provided the UK with a strong and stable political system. Governments, in the main, stay in office for full terms. It is not usual for governments to lose votes on legislation in the House of Commons. This compares to some countries where political instability has been the norm. When Italy used a fully proportional electoral system, the country was plagued with political weakness and instability.

The UK has also had long periods of government, which also may be seen as stabilising. The Blair government lasted 10 years, and Mrs Thatcher's government lasted for over 11 years. Both of these administrations have been able (with the help of large majorities) to implement the vast majority of their election manifestos. This might not have been possible had a different electoral system been in place.

UK government has normally comprised a single party and, again, the simple plurality system may be thanked for this. All governments since the end of the Second World War have been single-party governments. This situation contrasts sharply with countries that use proportional electoral systems. In Germany, for example, coalition governments are a permanent fixture. These systems may be less stable and the potential for political conflict inside the government is significant. The periods when coalition governments are being formed (often behind closed doors and in secret) are times of uncertainty. In the German general election of 2005, there was no clear result. Long negotiations between parties had to ensue in order to determine which would be in government.

It may be argued that single-party government is more accountable, in that there is only one party to blame if mistakes are made in carrying out public policy. The simple plurality system helps guard UK politics from coalition government where accountability is blurred and unclear. Furthermore, voters know who their MP is and can hold him or her to account in a general election. MPs have to put themselves forward for election every 4 or 5 years and cannot hide behind their party label if they have not been doing a good job. Any loss of this individual accountability of MPs would weaken the political system.

question

The UK's electoral system is easy to understand. Put simply, in a constituency, voters just put a cross beside their preferred candidate. The candidate with the most votes wins the seat. That candidate then becomes the Member of Parliament for that constituency until the next general election. The political party with the majority of seats in the House of Commons forms the government. There are no confusing ballot papers, no preferential voting and no complicated quotas for counting the votes which can characterise proportional electoral systems.

Most politicians believe that constituency representation is one of the key strengths of the UK political system. The link between the voter and his or her representative is crucially important. MPs deal with a variety of problems ranging from the state of the local schools to violent crime. They can often raise questions with the relevant minister in a parliamentary written question. It could be argued that the simple plurality system, based on small constituencies, helps preserve the link. Other voting systems might see this link weakened or lost altogether. The party list system, for example, affects constituency representation in that voters choose a party and not a candidate, so there is no direct connection between the voter and the elected representative.

e This response clearly answers the question. Both sides of the debate about electoral reform are tackled. The argument deals with both the strengths and weaknesses of the simple plurality system as well as referring to the strengths and weaknesses of particular alternative voting systems. As such there is a good demonstration of evaluative skills in this answer.

There is a good use of illustrative material, bringing in examples from abroad with an attempt to extrapolate outcomes for the UK political system. Clearly, higher level analytical skills are in evidence in this response.

Overall, this is a thorough answer which is both wide-ranging and analytical. It includes every significant factor and the candidate offers sophisticated evaluations of the different electoral systems.

Mark: 23 or 24/25

Total marks for question: 37/40

C-grade answer

(a) Proportional representation is an electoral system. This is where the seats that a party wins are equal to the votes that it wins. A party that wins 40% of the vote would get 40% of the seats.

e Although this answer addresses the question, it would not achieve full marks because it lacks precision. The first sentence appears to indicate that the candidate believes that proportional representation is a voting system. The second sentence is misleading and if it were not for the final sentence, where a working example is offered, it would remain unclear whether the candidate really understands the concept.

Mark: 2–3/5

(b) The list system has been introduced by the government for European elections. This system involves voting for a party and not a person. Whatever percentage of the vote is received by the party, that is the percentage of MEPs elected. Each party has a list of candidates.

AMS is where voters get two votes: one for a party and one for the representative. This allows for both constituencies and representation of smaller parties that might not be able to win a constituency seat. The system is used in Scotland.

e The candidate's description of the list system is fair. Although it does not include the proper name of the system, it does identify correctly the elections for which it is used. However, the candidate does not explain clearly the relation of party lists to how MEPs are elected. The grade-A candidate explained this relationship much more explicitly.

The second part of the response identifies the additional member system correctly as consisting of two parts, although it does not specify the different electoral systems used for each. The important concepts of constituency representation and (by inference) proportionality are also recognised. However, although the candidate identifies the place where the system is used, the precise institution (the Scottish Parliament) is not mentioned.

Overall, this response is not only qualitatively weaker but much shorter than the grade-A response. There are only 89 words, which is fewer than 50 words for each of the systems being described.

Mark: 4–5/10

(c) The current electoral system used in Britain is unfair to small parties. Labour and the Conservatives tend to do very well out of the first-past-the-post electoral system. Either of these have formed all recent governments. Parties such as the Liberal Democrats do not do as well. Electoral reform would lead to fairer representation for smaller political parties.

Reforming the voting system could also lead to coalition government. This could be seen as a fairer way of governing the country. Germany has had coalition governments for many years. Britain has had no coalition government since the Second World War.

On the other hand, the first-past-the-post electoral system has meant that Britain has had strong government for many years. The Thatcher and Blair governments could be said to have been strong governments. This is a good reason not to change the electoral system.

Coalitions may not be good for the political system. Parties might argue and there could be a risk of stalemate in government. Coalitions might also break down, leading to an increase in the number of elections required.

e This answer contains two valid points on either side of the debate about electoral reform. However, the candidate does not explain the points sufficiently well. The argument that coalition governments may be 'a fairer way of governing the country' is an assertion that requires development and justification. The lack of precision and detail in this answer prevents the candidate from gaining high marks for this question. The examples used are sparse, although that of the Liberal Democrats as an under-represented political party is a valid one. The grade-A answer extended the analysis to include parties that go totally unrepresented in national politics, such as UKIP and the Greens.

If the candidate had offered fuller explanations and made greater use of examples to back these up, the response would have gained more marks. Of equal importance, however, is the range covered by the response. Compare the number of points covered in the grade-A response to the points in the grade-C response.

Candidates have roughly 25 minutes to answer this question. This means that someone who can write 30 words in a minute might expect to produce a response of about 750 words. Even at a comparatively slow writing speed of 20 words a minute, a candidate might expect to write 500 words in the time allowed. This grade-C response is less than 200 words. While there is no guarantee that a long response will get a high mark, it is easier to predict that a shorter response will achieve a modest mark.

At least the candidate attempted to address both sides of the question. If the response had merely focused on one side of the debate, then the marks awarded would be limited further. Normally, high-level marks cannot be achieved for partial responses which do not cover the requirements of the question.

Mark: 9–10/25

Total mark for the question: 18/40

Question 4

Pressure groups

(a) Distinguish between promotional and sectional pressure groups. (5 marks)

(b) Explain the main differences between pressure groups and political parties. (10 marks)

(c) To what extent do pressure groups promote participation and responsive government? (25 marks)

Total: 40 marks

(a) This question requires you to distinguish between two different types of pressure group. Failure to address both aspects of the question could cost up to 4 of the 5 marks available.

(b) As with part (a), you are being asked to write about two groups: pressure groups and political parties. The key to achieving a high mark is to ensure that your answer addresses both of these fully, with relevant examples. If you address just one part, you will only be able to achieve half of the marks available.

(c) The key words in this question are 'to what extent'. They indicate that you must consider a number of arguments both for and against the notion that pressure groups promote participation and responsive government. Your conclusion should then make a balanced judgement, based on the arguments you have made in the rest of your answer. If you only look at one side of the debate, the maximum you can get is 10 or 11 out of 25, and even an excellent one-sided response will probably only get 13–14 marks, which would not place it in the grade-A mark band.

■ ■ ■

A-grade answer

(a) Promotional groups are those that represent a specific issue or a cause. An example of such a group is Friends of the Earth, which is concerned with the protection of the environment. Sectional groups promote or protect the interests of a specific group of people or interest. Examples of sectional groups include trade unions, such as the National Union of Teachers, and some professional associations, such as the British Medical Association, which represents the interests of doctors.

This answer gives enough information to be awarded full marks. It examines both types of pressure group mentioned in the question. The points are well explained and relevant examples are given.

Mark: 5/5

(b) One important difference is policy range. Pressure groups usually concentrate on one policy area or on a narrow field of issues. Greenpeace, for example, focuses its attention on matters to do with the protection of the environment. The Campaign for Nuclear Disarmament concentrates on policies concerning nuclear weapons and, more recently, on wider defence policy issues, but remains focused on a defined policy area. Political parties, by contrast, must have policies on a variety of issues because their aim is to wield political power in a number of policy areas. At a general election, political parties publish manifestos that cover issues such as the economy, welfare, transport and education.

Another difference between pressure groups and political parties relates to their aims. Pressure groups want to exert pressure on policy makers in order to achieve particular ends. Groups such as the National Farmers' Union therefore spend time lobbying decision-makers both in Westminster and in Brussels. As such, pressure groups do not seek elected power. Political parties, on the other hand, do seek power in order to carry out their policy objectives. At the core of a political party's agenda is the aim of getting into office; otherwise its policies cannot be turned into reality.

Political parties are accountable. In other words, they are held answerable for the actions of those who govern in their name. Politicians have to stand for election and, if they wish to continue in a representative capacity, for re-election. The governing party has to resubmit itself to the electorate after a certain period of time. Pressure groups are not accountable in the same way. Some pressure groups are not accountable at all because their leaders are not elected by the members of the group. Consequently, it can be argued that in this respect pressure groups are less democratic than political parties.

🖉 This is a good response that has the necessary range and depth. The candidate discusses three main differences between pressure groups and political parties. These differences are well explained and are illustrated with appropriate examples. Given the relatively short time available to complete these answers, the candidate rightly focuses on the key points that need to be made, without any repetition or wandering off the point. Such precision of written communication is essential when answering this type of question.

Mark: 9–10/10

(c) It may be argued that pressure groups enhance the political system because they are an additional form of participation. The level of this participation may vary; some individuals may be content to subscribe to a pressure group, while others may take a more active role. The Countryside Alliance encouraged its members to take an active part in its various activities, such as the protests against the ban on hunting with dogs.

Pressure groups enable citizens to participate in the period between elections. An example of this would be the many groups who came together under the 'Stop the War' banner in the run-up to the invasion of Iraq in 2003. This protest took place midway between the 2001 and 2005 general elections. May 2005 was the last occasion when voters were able to participate in a national election. Groups such as Liberty are working hard to gather support for their opposition to aspects of the Counter-Terrorism Bill in 2008 and the Terror Bill as well as protesting against the introduction of identity cards.

Many people support parties, such as the Greens, that currently have no MPs in the House of Commons. Environmental pressure groups enable such supporters to participate meaningfully in the political system, giving them a voice on issues that concern them.

The decline in the membership of political parties has been countered by an increase in the number and membership of pressure groups. It may be argued that pressure groups are now a more appropriate means of participation in the UK. The increase in the salience of single issue politics in the UK means that citizens are more willing to take part in pressure group activities such as a Greenpeace rally rather than commit time to supporting political parties.

Pressure groups also enhance government responsiveness. They are a measure of public opinion. This means that, on a range of issues, governments can gauge the views of the electorate, and it can be argued that governments are responsive to the views of the people. In the 1990s, following the Dunblane killings, the Snowdrop Campaign prompted the Major government and then the Blair administration to take action to further restrict gun ownership.

The issue focused on by the group is bound to affect the degree of government responsiveness. The issue needs to be salient to the public and the government needs to have some sympathy with it before it is likely to act. Clearly, environmental pressure groups such as Friends of the Earth find government much more responsive to their agenda given that the issue of climate change has dominated political agendas across the world.

Pressure groups may not necessarily enhance participation however. Some of the most successful groups in the UK are large business corporations. These groups do not provide for the participation of the general public. The numbers involved in influencing policy-makers are small. The Blair government was accused by many on the left of allowing big business too much access and influence. This angered many on the left because the Labour leadership appeared to be abandoning their traditional allies in the trade unions.

The nature and role of insider pressure groups may also be considered as not enhancing political participation. Many of these pressure groups work in secret, out of the public glare and far from public involvement. The leadership of the CBI in the late 1990s was accused of having too close a relationship with 10 Downing Street, both by its wider membership and individuals outside the organisation.

Government responsiveness is not assured. Even a pressure group which has received much media attention over a long period of time may find itself

unsuccessful in managing to change government policy. A clear example of this is Fathers 4 Justice, which, over a number of years, orchestrated a series of publicity stunts to raise the profile of the rights of fathers separated from their children. In spite of all this media attention, the group has been unsuccessful in achieving any significant change in family law that might have gone some way in meeting its ends.

Some groups behave in a way that directly challenges the democratic process. Those groups that engage in controversial, illegal or violent activities may be criticised in this respect. Some sections of the animal rights movement have resorted to actions that have put lives at risk. Some would argue that the activities of groups such as Greenpeace are also undemocratic (as in the case of the Brent Spa oil platform in the 1990s). Such activities are unlikely to enhance government responsiveness in a way that might be sympathetic to their cause.

e This is a full and balanced response which addresses the question directly; it would achieve nearly full marks. There are no rules about how many points you should make overall or the number of points you should include on each side (unless the question specifies this). You could get a grade A without necessarily making all of the above points, but clearly the more points you make, the greater the breadth of knowledge and understanding you will demonstrate to the examiner, as long as you explain each point well. Similarly, you should not be too concerned if you make more points on one side of the argument than the other. It may well be that your response contains four points in favour of a particular proposition and only two against. The key point is that you have demonstrated skills of evaluation (AO2) by offering arguments on both sides of a particular debate.

Mark: 23–24/25

Total mark for the question: 39/40

C-grade answer

(a) A promotional group looks to fight on issues such as health. Sectional groups are different because they want to fight for groups of individuals who have something in common, such as a job.

e Although this answer refers to both of the types of pressure group required by the question, it would not achieve full marks because the explanation lacks precision and no real examples are given.

Mark: 3/5

(b) There are two main differences between a pressure group and a political party. Parties want to get elected to power and therefore put up candidates in elections. Pressure groups, on the other hand, do not put up candidates in elections because they do not seek elected office. Pressure groups want to influence those in power, the politicians, by a variety of means. Another difference between pressure groups and political parties is the fact that pressure groups usually only have one aim and they confine themselves to that area of policy, such as Greenpeace and the environment. Political parties have ideas and plans on a wider range of issues such as defence, health and education as well as the environment.

🖉 This response is mainly held back to a grade C because of its limited range. It contains only two substantive points, whereas the grade-A answer contained three. However, if the candidate had explained these two points in more detail, and offered more examples to back them up, this response might have been worth more than a grade C. It is important to remember that the quality of your work is often as important as the quantity.

Mark: 4–5/10

(c) Pressure groups allow for extra participation. They therefore help people get more involved in politics. When people go on demonstrations or marches, such as against the Iraq war, they are getting involved in the political process in a way they might not otherwise. Participation is seen as a good sign that democracy is working.

Pressure groups can be seen as an additional type of representation. The big political parties often do not reflect the opinions of some individuals, especially those with strong opinions on certain issues. By definition, the parties need to have opinions on a wide range of issues and cannot devote too much time to individual ones. These opinions do not get aired in parliament. Pressure groups can be seen as a way of giving these issues a voice in the country.

Governments will listen to the arguments of pressure groups because they represent the opinions of their members who are also voters. As such they enhance the responsiveness of government. This may be particularly true as a general election approaches. Indeed, groups may deliberately time their activities in order to influence government ahead of an election. The fuel protests of 2000 took place in the autumn before the election expected in the spring of 2001.

Pressure groups may also provide expert advice to the government. This can be in the form of data or reports that are put together and then published and sent to ministers. This means that they are providing information from the front line, as it were, and those in power might find it useful when making future policy decisions. Once again, this demonstrates that pressure group activity may enhance the responsiveness of governments.

Pressure groups hinder democracy because they are unaccountable. Many groups do not elect their leaders and are therefore not answerable to the people who pay their subscription fees to the pressure group itself. This means that ordinary members have no way of getting rid of their leaders if they become unpopular or take decisions for which there may be disapproval. This could be seen as reducing the amount of participation in the UK political system.

Some pressure groups may only be listened to because they have a lot of money. Such groups may have more influence over the political process and this could be seen to be undemocratic. In a democracy, the amount of money a group has should not determine how much power and influence it has.

This response attempts to be balanced, but the stronger points tend to be in favour of the proposition. The final paragraph can be seen to be irrelevant to the question. There is evidence, however, that the candidate is trying to bend pre-learned material to suit the question and these points might have more easily fitted into a question about pressure groups and democracy.

There are fewer relevant points made in this response than in the grade-A answer and its explanations are not as insightful. It also offers very few examples of the activities of particular pressure groups.

Mark: 11/25

Total mark for the question: 22/40